Lovely

{Think about Such Things}

Encouragement from Philippians 4:8

TINA KRAUSE

BARBOUR
PUBLISHING

{ Contents }

Introduction 7

Multiple Choice: True or False? 9

Honesty Is Honorable 31

It's Always Right to Do Right 51

Purity: The Christian's Holy Grail 73

How Lovely 93

A Good Report Equals a Good Reputation 115

Virtue: Our Standard of Excellence 137

Give Praise Where Praise Is Due 157

Seriously. . .Think about It 179

{ Introduction }

How's your thought life? Have you ever experienced an overwhelming life issue or a day so bad that every thought resonated negativity? You're not alone.

Philippians 4:8 (KJV) states: "Finally, brethren, whatsoever things are true, whatsoever things are honest, whatsoever things are just, whatsoever things are pure, whatsoever things are lovely, whatsoever things are of good report; if there be any virtue, and if there be any praise, think on these things."

But how do we focus on whatever is lovely while living in a problem-permeated world? Each section of this book is devoted to one of the characteristics listed in Philippians 4:8 to help us implement these godly attributes into our daily lives.

Whatever circumstance you face, be encouraged. Loveliness is achievable when we begin to think about such things.

> *Where I found truth, there found I my God, who is the truth itself.*
>
> SAINT AUGUSTINE

Multiple Choice:
True or False?

Walking in Truth

*I have no greater joy than to hear that
my children are walking in the truth.*

3 John 1:4 NIV

*Y*ears ago, Trish and her husband vacationed in
Jamaica. While strolling the streets of Ocho Rios,
they chatted with the locals. There they met Lora, a
young single working mother. Before parting, Trish
asked for her address so they could mail packages
to her and her young son. For years, Trish and Lora
exchanged letters and Trish mailed boxes brimming
with items Lora and her son could use. In many of her
letters, Trish shared her faith in Christ and the truth
of God's Word.

Then Lora moved, and they lost contact. Years
passed, but Trish continued to pray for Lora's
salvation though she thought she'd never know if her
prayers were answered—until one unexpected letter
arrived postmarked from Jamaica. It read: *"My dear*

friend Trish: I have good news. I asked Jesus Christ into my heart and I am living a Christian life. I have joined a church, and the people there give me and my son much love and support. I have a lot to learn, but I wanted to tell you about this wonderful change in my life. Thank you for sharing Jesus with me so long ago."

Can you imagine Trish's excitement? Tears of joy dampened the handwritten page. For the first time Trish personalized the words of John: "I have no greater joy than to hear that my children are walking in the truth."

Moms experience the joy of holding their children for the first time, seeing them crawl or take a first step. They beam with pride when their child graduates from college or achieves a milestone. They praise the Lord to witness their adult children serving God.

There is no greater joy than to see our children–spiritual or physical–walking with God. And God has no greater joy than to see us walking in His truth.

But It's Only a White Lie

I will always speak the truth
and refuse to tell a lie.

PROVERBS 8:7 CEV

There's one in every family or fellowship. Someone whose words you always question: Is what they're telling me true or false? You want to believe her; you long to trust him, but can you? That question emerges every time you have a conversation.

Some people, even Christians, believe that embellishing the truth is acceptable. After all, what harm are a few exaggerations or omissions to a story or event? They think the "little white lie" myth absolves them from telling the whole truth. But the Bible is clear: little white lies are lies. Embrace the truth and refuse to lie.

Think about it—all cult religions proclaim an element of biblical truth taken out of context, stretched or manipulated to mold the minds of unsuspecting people. Cult leaders stand before listening ears as they drum out misquoted scriptures and half-truths. And the results are devastating.

A. J. Gossip, author and professor of theology, put it this way: "Do not burn false fire upon God's altar; do not pose and pretend, either to Him or to yourself, in your religious exercises; do not say more than you mean, or use exaggerated language that goes beyond the facts."

Unlike the religious leaders who twist and distort the truth, God is not a dictator; He's a loving, compassionate, faithful Father. While the devil manipulates, God gives us the freedom to choose the truth or falsehoods.

In the above scripture King Solomon, the voice of wisdom, vowed to speak truth and detest lies. That's a choice we all make.

Do we speak the truth, or do we allow white lies to spawn self-deception and misdirection? The choice is ours.

Ye shall know the truth,
and the truth shall make you free.
JOHN 8:32 KJV

Georgia thought she was right about most, if not all, things. Personal conflicts were always someone else's fault. She blamed her parents for her personality problems and life issues. Often, she misunderstood a friend's intentions or distorted what she perceived as truth in her conversations and experiences with others. As a result, she alienated herself from the very people who wanted to help or befriend her.

Coworkers, friends, and family readily admitted that Georgia suffered from self-deception, pride, and an uncompromising personality. She rejected the truth about herself, and–in doing so–she grew into a depressed, lonely, cynical person.

So how can we know the truth that Jesus talked about in the book of John? Moreover, how can that truth free us? God loves a teachable, humble spirit. But most of us dislike being told we're wrong. The truth invokes more of an "ouch" than an "aah," because accepting it really stings.

Regardless, Christian women who receive the truth as an "aha" moment or a godly epiphany that transforms their thinking, thrive in their walks with God.

Remember when you chose to follow Christ? You didn't exactly jump up, cheer, and applaud when you realized that you were a sinner in need of salvation; yet, that "godly sorrow" led you to repent and embrace God's forgiveness through Christ (2 Corinthians 7:10). The result? Freedom. Freedom from guilt and sin. Freedom to walk in newness of life with a blank slate, unstained from your sinful past.

God accepts us as we are but loves us far too much to leave us that way. And although the truth hurts, it liberates!

Call the Comforter

*I {Jesus} will send you the Spirit
who comes from the Father and shows
what is true. The Spirit will help you
and will tell you about me.*

JOHN 15:26 CEV

Have you ever found yourself in a quandary,
undecided about what to do or how to go about it?
Perhaps you are considering a move, a job change,
or how to begin a difficult undertaking, and you
desperately need the input of a trusted friend or
family member. You fear mistakes, and the thought
of making the wrong decision and living with the
consequences and risks involved paralyzes you,
preventing you from taking any action at all.

Often, a praying friend provides godly insight or
a confirmation to what you've already considered. At
peace, you move forward. But what about those times
you struggle to make a solid determination? What

do you do when the answer is about as clear as eye cataracts, and confusion blurs your vision?

Jesus promised us the Holy Spirit. He resides within us all of the time, wherever we are. The Greek translation of Holy Spirit is the word *parakletos*, which means "the one called to one's side." He is God's Spirit who provides all wisdom, truth, counsel, and strength. He comforts, intercedes on our behalf, and gives us what we need when we need it. He not only walks alongside us, He dwells within us.

Jesus assures us that the Holy Spirit will show us what's true. The Holy Spirit is the helper we need most, and He's just a whisper away.

Are you struggling with an overwhelming decision? Do you want the truth revealed to your searching heart? Have you run out of answers and have nowhere to turn?

The Holy Spirit is available to those who have placed their faith in Christ. He's right where you are right now. Call on Him; He's waiting to hear from you.

What's the Truth about Heaven?

> *There are many rooms in my Father's house.*
> *I wouldn't tell you this, unless it was true.*
> *I am going there to prepare a place for each of you.*
>
> JOHN 14:2 CEV

*I*s heaven a real place or merely a spiritual mirage based on fictional concepts of winged cherubs perched on wispy clouds and a white-haired Saint Peter sitting at the golden gates with scroll and pen in hand? What can the Christian expect when he or she passes from this world into eternity?

God is not only the author of truth, he is *all* truth. In other words, it is impossible for Him to lie. Jesus promised His disciples and followers that—along with streets of pure gold and scenes unequaled to anything we have ever witnessed on earth—God, even at this very moment, is constructing living quarters for us. And not just residential stately mansions; rather, heavenly palatial homes built by the Master

Carpenter himself. Literal homes custom built to last an eternity in the celestial city called heaven.

Heaven is a real place far beyond anything we could ever think or imagine. The apostle Paul reminded the Corinthian church about heaven, saying: " 'No eye has seen, no ear has heard, no mind has conceived' what God has prepared for those who love him" (1 Corinthians 2:9 NIV).

Jesus assured us that if the truth about heaven were false, He would have said so.

Rather, He affirms that after we ask Jesus to forgive our sins and enter our hearts and lives, we can confidently know that this earth is not our permanent home. Heaven awaits every Christian. . .and it is real. That's the truth.

What or Who Cut in on You?

You were running a good race.
Who cut in on you to keep you
from obeying the truth?

GALATIANS 5:7 NIV

Many parents can relate to this question from Galatians. "You aced history last semester, and now you got a D? What happened?"

Or how about that diet? For months you adhere to your weight-loss program. You're shedding pounds slowly but steadily, and you're determined. Then an unexpected situation arises. Your elderly mom is hospitalized so you spend hours at her bedside, consulting with doctors and keeping family and friends updated. Suddenly, eating cafeteria hospital food is the highlight of your day. By the time you get home, you're exhausted. No time for exercise as you catch up with unattended duties. Instantly your diet is sabotaged.

Paul often refers to the Christian life as a foot race. Runners know how important consistency is. Pacing, timing, and finding your rhythm are essential to running a good race. Yet at any time, something or someone can cut you off. You lose your timing when your shoe unties, forcing you to stop, bend down, and start running again. Someone cuts in front of you and throws off your rhythm. In an effort to catch up, you run faster than you should and lose your pace.

Spiritually, our consistency falters when we allow people, circumstances, or things to divert us from the truth of God's Word. Bad influences tempt us to act or do something against our convictions. Work pressures weaken our wills, and we lash out in anger.

Daily life oozes with people and circumstances that derail us from obeying God's Word. Yet God forgives and redirects our course.

Has something or someone distracted you from following the truth? Confess what happened and get back in the race.

Live Truthfully

*Rather, let our lives lovingly express
truth {in all things, speaking truly,
dealing truly, living truly}.
Enfolded in love, let us grow up in every way.*

EPHESIANS 4:15 AMP

Karen left the store, and when she returned home, she realized the store had bagged an item for which she hadn't paid. Instead of returning with payment for the item, she justified her dishonesty by thinking, *Well, it's not my fault the clerk was so careless.*

Jennifer, a new employee, approached a seasoned coworker to ask for an honest assessment. "Do you think my work on this project needs improvement?" Swamped with work and wanting to avoid disruption, the coworker said, "No, you're doing great! Don't worry about it." Instead of offering constructive criticism, her coworker lied.

Paul's letter to the Ephesians exhorts us to lovingly

express the truth in every area of our lives. Notice the emphasis on "lovingly." The spirit behind what we say or do determines whether or not the truth we convey is from the heart of God or our own sinful nature.

It is God's love that compels us to obey His commands and the leading of the Holy Spirit. His love motivates us to do the right thing even when we're tempted to justify our actions like Karen did.

Jennifer's coworker missed the opportunity to help her; instead, she opted for the easier path.

Walking in the truth is hard work. Listening to the still, small voice of the Spirit and obeying Him is often an inconvenience. But as we lovingly speak, deal, and live in truth, we grow and please the One whom we serve.

The Road to Bartonville, the Way to Truth

Jesus told him, "I am the way,
the truth, and the life. No one can
come to the Father except through me."

JOHN 14:6 NLT

*L*ost on unfamiliar roads, Beth stopped at a small country gas station for directions. "Excuse me," she inquired. "Which way is Blaine Street?"

The owner hesitated for a moment and asked, "Where you headed? Blaine Street runs in different directions!"

"I'm going to 1050 Blaine."

"Ya sure?" he replied, swishing chewing tobacco to one side of his mouth.

"Yes," she answered.

"Then ya better go through the next town, 'cuz there's only one way to get there–through Bartonville. Only after you pass through Bartonville will you find that address!"

Some religions claim that their doctrines are the true way to achieve fulfillment and eternal security, but Jesus said that He alone is the way to salvation. The world thinks many roads lead to God. But Jesus is the only way to the Father. Jesus alone died for our sins to provide forgiveness. Then He rose from the grave and is alive today.

Like Beth, we are lost on the unfamiliar roads of life. So we seek direction. Sometimes we receive false information; other times we find some unlikely individual who tells us the truth and helps us find our way. There was only one way to reach the address Beth sought—through Bartonville. And there's only one way to reach God—through accepting Jesus Christ as our Lord and Savior. Although the Blaine Street of religion runs in different directions, the targeted destination on our pathway to God and eternal security rests on receiving and knowing Christ.

Have you ever asked Jesus to come into your life? If not, Bartonville is just a prayer away.

Our Choice:
True or False Teachings?

*{These weak women will listen to anybody who
will teach them}; they are forever inquiring and
getting information, but are never able to arrive
at a recognition and knowledge of the Truth.*

2 TIMOTHY 3:7 AMP

*W*hat in the world was the apostle Paul telling
Timothy, a young missionary? Did Paul dislike
women? How condescending! What was he thinking?

Apparently some false teachings were circulating
throughout the church that was under Timothy's care.
These teachings opposed the essential truths of the
Christian faith, and many believers–especially some
of the women–believed whatever the false teachers
said. These ladies attended church and pretended to
love God, but they accepted the concept that sound
doctrine was unnecessary. Instead, they embraced
only the teachings they wanted to hear–the ones that
assured them that living a sinful life was just fine.

Do you know of anyone like that? Maybe she attends every Bible study, church service, and women's retreat. Diligently, she jots notes while listening to the message. She seems eager to learn all she can; yet, apart from the church she lives an ungodly lifestyle. She knows "the way" but seldom walks in the precepts of God's Word. She claims to know God but exhibits a fruitless life. Justifying her bad behavior, she simply says that God forgives. Self-deceived, she continues to conform to her own selfish, worldly desires.

When we arrive at a true recognition and knowledge of the truth, we desire to live differently. We want to please God and adhere to His Word and the leading of His Holy Spirit. Women of God reject any idea or teaching that is in opposition to what the scriptures teach. And that's the truth of the matter.

> *God's way is perfect.*
> *All the* Lord's *promises prove true.*
> Psalm 18:30 nlt

Have you ever been the recipient of a broken promise? It's heartbreaking. That's why one wise mom once made this phrase her personal mantra: "Promise only what I can deliver. Then deliver more than I promised."

In the moment, it's so easy to say, "Yes, I promise," especially to our kids. Sometimes we just want to silence their persistent inquiries; other times we have good intentions, but circumstances unfold that make delivering the promise difficult. The fact is we are imperfect humans living in an imperfect world.

The above scripture assures us that God's way is true perfection. Every promise, from big to small, is true. He didn't promise it unless He could deliver. And He always delivers as we faithfully stand on, cleave to, and believe in His promises.

Does that mean that we get everything we pray for? No, but He answers every prayer in His way and according to His timetable. After all, do we give our daughter everything she wants? Do we allow our teen to do everything he asks? Nope! A good parent realizes that some things are detrimental to the health, safety, or spiritual well-being of her child. God is the same with His children.

His promises are true; it is impossible for God to break them. And He desires the same of us. When we promise, we commit to someone or something. To break a promise is to forfeit our credibility and trustworthiness. Repeated broken promises damage our reputations as women of integrity and truthfulness. Soon our kids, coworkers, and family doubt our word.

Broken promises hurt, but it's never too late to trust the One who will never fail us and become someone whose promises are true.

{
*An honest heart seeks to please God
in all things and offend Him in none.*
A. W. PINK
}

Honesty Is Honorable

Honest, Guilt-Free Living

Yes, what joy for those whose
record the LORD has cleared of guilt,
whose lives are lived in complete honesty!

PSALM 32:2 NLT

Advertisers boast about their low-calorie, guilt-free chocolate brownies and mouthwatering pasta dishes. If you're watching your calories, the prospect of eating these delectables without guilt is exciting! In fact, it brings relief to the dieter who's been munching on rabbit food too long.

The same is true after we experience the joy of God's forgiveness when we ask for salvation through Jesus Christ. No more guilt! The record of sinfulness is erased as we stride forward in newness of life.

From that day forward, every true believer strives to live, talk, think, and act honestly. No more lies or half-truths. No more deception and distortion of facts. We want to please God, and that means living in complete honesty.

Should we momentarily stumble and guilt creeps in, God lifts us to our feet with His forgiveness and love, and we move forward.

When we stumble–and we will–it's important to learn from our mistakes and not make the same ones again. True repentance brings honest deliverance from past sins that once placed us in a stranglehold of guilt and torment. Christians are freed from all former bondages that prevented us from living honest, holy lives. Why? Because the King of kings resides within us and empowers us to walk according to His Word. We don't need to try to live honestly on our own. The Holy Spirit is our constant guide, leading us in truth and honesty.

So we can boast of God's power, not our own, as we live guilt free. And who can say that about their daily diets?

Quiet and Peaceful Honesty

For kings, and for all that are in authority;
that we may lead a quiet and peaceable
life in all godliness and honesty.

1 TIMOTHY 2:2 KJV

Are you a mom? Employer? Worship or Bible class leader? You may not be royalty, but if God has placed you in any position of authority, the above verse pertains to you.

Consider this, Mom: You race home from work and notice the laundry still litters the utility-room floor. You toss in a load while starting dinner. Meanwhile, your teenage daughter follows you, venting about her "horrible day" at school, and your son yells in the background that he needs help with his homework. As you inform your daughter in a not-so-quiet-and-peaceable tone that your day wasn't exactly birthed in the Magic Kingdom, Hubby walks in with the bad news that his car broke down. "Now we're down to one car. I don't know what we're going to do," he moans.

Images of escape infiltrate your thinking: You. Alone. Racing down the street, driving away from your wifely and motherly duties in your family's one and only functioning car. At this point, godliness and honesty rank low on your life list.

If you are one who has people–little or otherwise– who depend on you, then you've had similar feelings and frustrations. We long to run away from it all.

The apostles lived a rough life, traveling from one town to another as God directed them. They underwent persecutions and problems; yet, Paul exhorted the young minister Timothy that those in authority should strive to live a quiet, peaceable life with all godliness and honesty. For us, that means living in all godliness and honesty even when the "quiet and peaceable" are only accessible in a car driven swiftly away from the chaos!

Is Honesty a Lost Attribute?

They did not require an accounting from those to whom they gave the money to pay the workers, because they acted with complete honesty.

2 Kings 12:15 niv

Do you know honest women, fair in all of their dealings? Are there honorable people with whom you work, who are worthy of your trust? Do you know people of integrity? Or do you think that honesty is a lost attribute today?

In the Old Testament the priests set up a special repair fund for maintenance of the temple. The Israelites placed donations in a large chest. When the chest filled, King Joash's financial secretary and high priest counted the money and put it into bags. Then they gave it to the construction superintendent to pay the carpenters, stonemasons, quarrymen, and dealers (2 Kings 12:8–12). Amazingly, the king and high priest never asked for an account of where the money went to repair the temple, because the workers had proved their honesty and integrity repeatedly.

Unfortunately, that's an uncommon practice today. Can you imagine handing over a sack of money to your plumber, roofer, or construction worker with that kind of trust? No wise woman would do that without sound assurance that the laborer was trustworthy.

The same is true in our personal lives. If we've ever fudged on a number, taken office supplies, discredited a coworker, lied about taking a day off, or done anything worthy of close scrutiny, then we've violated our integrity as well as an honest work ethic. Complete honesty–a lost attribute? Not for the Christian woman.

*But you desire honesty from the womb,
teaching me wisdom even there.*

PSALM 51:6 NLT

Nana, why do your arms jiggle like Jell-O when you wave good-bye?" three-year-old Alex asked. "Uncle Jeff is so tall, is he a real giant?" Kaitlyn inquires. Children are amazingly—and sometimes painfully—honest. Without a thought they'll blurt out whatever question or comment occupies their little minds.

King David said that God desires honesty and teaches us wisdom from the womb. Wow! Expectant moms and new mothers, can you wrap your minds around that? Even as your baby forms silently in the womb, God teaches him or her wisdom. Your newborn, cradled in your arms, already possesses the attribute of honesty!

It is only as we grow older that our unpretentious honesty dilutes in a mixture of peer pressures, pride, fears, and frustrations. Older children lie for fear of consequences. Teens embarrass easily and desire to fit in, so they succumb to peer pressure. Adults dislike hearing the truth, especially if it pains their egos or discredits their ideas. Yet no matter the age, God desires honesty. He provides us with wisdom from the onset of our lives to learn honesty with God, ourselves, and others.

Jesus said that we must approach Him as a little child. A small child is open, honest, trusting, and teachable. We must be "born again," not physically but spiritually. When we ask Him into our lives, we become babes in Christ, ready and eager to nurse on the milk of His Word. And just as our child basks in our applause for the smallest accomplishments, we desire to please our Father with wisdom and honesty.

The Answer to Unanswered Prayer

*Then your light will shine like the dawning sun,
and you will quickly be healed. Your honesty
will protect you as you advance, and the glory
of the* LORD *will defend you from behind.*

ISAIAH 58:8 CEV

What a promise! Yet this verse comes with a condition.

Here's what happened in the previous passages.
God's people were complaining. (Ever been there?)
They asked God why He was unimpressed with their
fasting and sacrifices. They performed acts of penance
and prayed, but God, it seemed, never noticed. (Ever
feel like that?)

Finally God gave them a bitter dose of the truth.
He basically said, "Here's why I haven't answered
you: You live in evil pleasures and oppress your
workers with dishonesty. Yet you bow like reeds in the
wind and wear sackcloth and ashes while you're doing
it. You call that fasting?"

He then explained what true prayer and fasting is—to stop hurting others and treat them honestly and fairly. To share provisions and clothing with the poor and needy. Last, to help our relatives and not hide from them! (Ever done that?)

Isaiah says if we adhere to honesty, our lights will shine as the dawning sun and we will be healed.

Our honesty will serve as a shield of protection as we live our lives, while God's glory watches our backs. Did you notice? God will watch your back! And He will hear and answer your prayers.

Who wouldn't want that? (What's more, who doesn't need it?)

Prayer, a Clear Conscience, and an Honorable Life

Keep praying for us, for we are convinced that we have a good (clear) conscience, that we want to walk uprightly and live a noble life, acting honorably and in complete honesty in all things.

HEBREWS 13:48 AMP

Can you recall how many times you've asked a close Christian friend or church prayer warrior to "keep praying" for you or someone near to you? You realize that their prayers are what sustain you during hard times.

Edna was a praying woman. If God placed someone on her heart, she'd stop whatever she was doing to pray for them, though she knew nothing about their circumstances. Later, she'd discover how that person needed help at the very time Edna had prayed. What would we do without our faithful praying brothers and sisters in the Lord?

The Christian is no stranger to temptations and trials. We live in a sinful world, inundated with people whose standards and mind-sets oppose the teachings of Christ. Yet with the prayer support of fellow believers, coupled with our personal relationship with Jesus, we can walk through this troubled world with a clear conscience and a desire to continue to walk and live honorably.

Hebrews echoes our deepest personal request and heartfelt desire. To consistently walk with God is not only noteworthy but honorable. From returning overpaid change to a cashier to telling the truth despite the consequences, honesty is, as the familiar axiom says, "the best policy."

To live an honorable life is to live an honest one. No false facades, just a clear conscience upheld by praying friends.

LORD, *you are searching for honesty.*
You struck your people, but they paid no
attention. You crushed them, but they refused
to be corrected. They are determined,
with faces set like stone; they have refused to repent.

JEREMIAH 5:3 NLT

How many times do I have to tell you?" we ask with
a grimace after repeating the same instructions to our
kids to do the same task or adhere to the same rule for
the umpteenth time. "When will you learn?"

We teach them, and they forget. We instruct, and
they don't listen. We nag, and they still don't listen.
We discipline, and even then they swiftly return to
their old ways the next day. "Lose the attitude!" we
chide, while they stomp away in anger. Frustrating,
isn't it?

God's kids are similar. We think we're right. We
set our faces like stone and refuse to budge until He

has no choice but to allow us to have our way and bear the consequences. Rebellion stinks, especially in the nostrils of our loving, powerful, omnipotent God. And God is the perfect parent!

Just as we search for obedience and honesty from our children, God seeks the same of us. "When will she learn?" He must ask. "What will it take?"

Elisabeth Elliot, missionary wife to Jim Elliot who was killed on the mission field, said: "Let us beware of rebellion against the Lord. Circumstances are of His choosing, because He wants to bless us, to lead us out of Egypt, that is, out of ourselves. Settle the complaint with God, and it will settle other things."

The Lord is in search of honesty: our honesty with Him, with ourselves, and with others. On the other hand, our hardened hearts and misplaced determination lead us back into Egypt and spiritual bondage.

When will we learn? When we honestly seek honesty.

Never pay back evil with more evil.
Do things in such a way that everyone
can see you are honorable.

ROMANS 12:17 NLT

*W*hat are some outward expressions of honorable thinking? For one, the Bible admonishes us never to play payback. If someone falsely accuses you, do you falsely accuse her? If an acquaintance claims your Tupperware bowl belongs to her, do you keep her cake pan? If a friend betrays you, do you think of ways to betray her? Not according to scripture.

Honorable thinking gives way to an honorable attitude and honorable acts. *Webster's New World Dictionary* defines honorable as "worthy of being honored; of good reputation; respectable; having or showing a sense of right and wrong; characterized by honesty and integrity; upright."

If someone publically takes credit for what you

did behind the scenes, let her. God knows, and He will reward you accordingly. If people despise you, pray for them. In other words, conquer evil with good as the Bible instructs in Romans 12:24.

Years ago a familiar Christian trend was the "What would Jesus do?" question. Pastors preached about it; Christians donned bracelets with the inscription WWJD. The question is worth remembering at the very moment we want to lash out and return evil for evil. What's the honorable thing to do? Is what I'm thinking or doing Christlike?

Jesus is the epitome of honorable thoughts, words, and deeds. We possess the same Spirit He did while He walked among us, and that empowers us to make the right choices.

The rewards of an honorable person are without measure. After all, who can buy respect or a good reputation? And who doesn't value integrity and honesty in others? It's something to consider when we're tempted to return evil for evil.

Look and See:
Am I Honorable?

*We are careful to be honorable before
the Lord, but we also want everyone
else to see that we are honorable.*

2 Corinthians 8:24 nlt

Is it vain or boastful to want others to think we are
honorable? We yearn to exhibit honorable thoughts
and behavior before God, but should we desire that
others notice our good attributes?

Perhaps the answer lies in what characteristics we
seek in a friend. We desire someone with whom we
can share our deepest thoughts and feelings. We want
a friend who will love us despite our shortcomings.
She is the type of person we can depend on for
prayer and godly counsel. We share a mutual trust,
respect, and admiration for each other. A true friend
recognizes and applauds our gifts, accomplishments,
and aspirations. She forgives our faults. In a word,
she's honorable.

If those characteristics are what we look for, wouldn't others look for the same qualities in us?

It is honorable to be aboveboard in everything we say and do, and to avoid hypocrisy or deceit. Not just before God but before others, because the world is watching. Unbelievers want to know if Christians are genuine—if we walk the talk, or talk only and act differently. The old axiom says: "Your life may be the only Bible some people read."

That's why Paul exhorted believers to use caution and exhibit honesty and honorable traits to the world and to one another. We are walking, talking examples—a representation of the very One who sacrificed His life to make us free. We owe it to Him. And we owe it to the lost world He died to save.

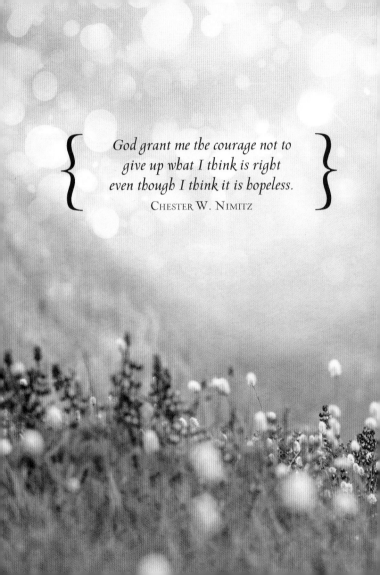

{ *God grant me the courage not to give up what I think is right even though I think it is hopeless.* }

CHESTER W. NIMITZ

It's Always
Right to Do Right

No Excuses

And he {Hezekiah} did that which
was right in the sight of the LORD,
according to all that David his father did.

2 KINGS 18:3 KJV

What do you expect, knowing the kind of parents I had?" Jodie lamented to a friend. Jodie's childhood had been far from a Norman Rockwell scene. Her divorced parents were alcoholics, and she'd raised herself as well as her younger siblings. Growing up, she'd had no rules, no structure, no love. So as a young adult she searched for love in all the wrong places. She eventually married and became the same type of mother that her mom was to her.

Hezekiah had a terrible father, Ahaz. Yet the Bible records that at twenty-five years old, Hezekiah was the most righteous king since King David. The first act he enforced after he assumed the throne was to destroy all the pagan altars and images. He restored

Solomon's temple and reigned with a passion to please the Lord. At a time when Judah's existence was threatened, he ruled with a godly attitude and concern for the people.

Using your poor upbringing or less-than-perfect childhood as an excuse to succumb to thoughts, actions, and words that displease the Lord or taint your witness isn't acceptable. We can choose a better way. We have biblical examples of people who were mistreated, abused, neglected, and shunned, yet grew to become young men and women of faith, determined to do what was right in God's eyes.

God desires to use you. Allow your trials to become the very vehicles God uses to touch others with His love.

Some people are blessed with a godly heritage; others are not. Either way, we make our own choices. Choose to do right.

We're Not Mountain Goats

Then you will understand what is right, just, and fair, and you will find the right way to go.

PROVERBS 2:9 NLT

Here's a profound thought. Are you ready? We're not mountain goats. Mountain goats can scale the highest mountaintops, surefooted and secure. They have the ability to navigate impossible crevices and dangerous jagged edges. We, on the other hand, lose our footing in life and often stumble from the mountaintop to the valley in an instant. That's when we need prayer and a close friend for a hand up.

Darlene was one of those friends. Nina had been in a slump for some time as one life onslaught after another plunged her into the valley of despair. Others simply said: "It'll be okay," or with an insincere flippancy replied, "I'll be praying for you!"

But Nina's friend Dar took the time and effort to offer help from her heart. She e-mailed Nina with pep talks each morning. She not only gave encouragement, she listened and understood how Nina felt, cognizant of how long she had faced ongoing problems. Dar was direct yet loving with her friend, and Nina absorbed her compassion and wisdom like black absorbs sunlight.

It's hard to see clearly in the valley. We lose our focus and direction, while frustration and discouragement tempt us to quit. We question ourselves and wonder, *What in the world happened?*

Evangelist Billy Graham said: "The Christian life is not a constant high. I have my moments of deep discouragement. I have to go to God in prayer with tears in my eyes and say, 'O God, forgive me,' or 'Please help me.'"

In her despair, Nina kept praying, and God bolstered her through a caring friend. And with that, like the verse states, she found the right way to go.

It Takes Practice

Learn to do right; seek justice.
Defend the oppressed. Take up the cause
of he fatherless; plead the case of the widow.
ISAIAH 1:17 NIV

If you're a mom, you know how kids imitate. They learn from our actions, words, and attitudes. We teach them to say "please" and "thank you" at the appropriate times; they learn boundaries according to our consistency in enforcing house rules and our loving discipline. But if we let them, they'll take advantage of situations to get their own way in our moments of weakness.

Here the Bible gives us some clear-cut instructions. First and foremost? "Learn to do right." Ahem. Learn? Shouldn't we just know? Sure, we might *know*, but *doing* is an apple from a different tree.

We are all born with sinful natures that need salvation through Christ. After we accept Him, the

Holy Spirit resides inside to *teach* us to do what's right. Learning is an ongoing process because, like a child, we're selfish by nature. We want our own way in our own timing. So the practice of doing what's right is essential in our walk with Christ.

Remember when you learned the first notes of a musical instrument? You had to practice repeatedly until you finally mastered them and were ready for the next level. Doing right is much like learning an instrument. At first we're awkward, stumbling to hit the mark correctly. But after we learn to live uprightly, our spiritual fingers flow with beauty and grace. It becomes second nature, much like our kids finally saying "please" and "thank you" after repeated instruction from us.

Isaiah directs us to learn to do, think, and act right. After that, all the rest follows.

Act Right;
Speak with Love

*We have spoken the truth, and God's power
has worked in us. In all our struggles we
have said and done only what is right.*

2 CORINTHIANS 6:7 CEV

The apostle Paul conveyed a message to the
Corinthian church: speak the truth in love; it's the
right thing to do! Be examples, he said, so that no one
will ever be held back from finding the Lord because
of the way you act (2 Corinthians 6:3–5).

Paul walked the talk. He was unjustly accused,
he faced angry mobs, he was imprisoned and beaten
and suffered every kind of hardship; yet, he never
crumbled under the natural instincts of a carnal
nature. He didn't lash out in anger or plan revenge.
He avoided faultfinding and backstabbing. Rather, he
spoke the truth of God's Word with a compassionate,
loving heart. He loved his enemies the way God loved
them.

Whenever we speak the truth, someone *will* get angry. Count on it. Our first reaction is to get defensive. But there's a better way–God's. Rather than personalizing how someone treats us, consider their past and what they may have gone through–or may be presently going through. Then ask yourself honestly, "Did I speak the truth in love? Or did I inwardly try to straighten them out? Was my speech meant to hurt more than help?"

Regardless of how others treat us, we are to patiently endure. Does that mean we become doormats? No! Christians are designed to exemplify Christ and His teachings, and Jesus was no doormat. He stood for what was right. Unafraid, He preached the Gospel to all people–from top religious leaders to harlots and outcasts, and He did it with love. That's the way God works, and with His help and power we can do the same.

Who Is Just?

Noah was a just man and perfect in his generations, and Noah walked with God.
GENESIS 6:9 KJV

Who is a just person? Someone who is honest? Dependable? Fair and impartial? Someone who is righteous and opposed to injustice? She or he is a person every woman looks for in a spouse or a friend.

Noah must have made a wonderful husband, father, and friend because of two essential spiritual criteria: he was just, and he walked with God. Do our peers think the same of us?

Let's face it, no one wants to appear before an unjust judge or find themselves at the mercy of an uncaring teacher or a quack doctor. We hope to trust the people in charge to exhibit fair and equal treatment. We hire attorneys with integrity, and we vote for reputable, dependable government officials–or at least we try.

The Lord looks for the same in us. He desires modern-day Noahs who love Him enough to obey His every command, whether or not we understand His leading. He wants women of God who are just, dependable, loving, and fair—women who guard themselves from gossip while giving others the benefit of the doubt.

Noah walked with God. It's only when we, too, walk with God that we begin to exhibit all of those characteristics and more.

So the next time you wonder, *Who is a just person?*, gaze in the mirror and with assurance say, "With God's help, I am."

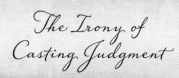

The Irony of
Casting Judgment

Don't condemn others, and God won't condemn you. God will be as hard on you as you are on others! He will treat you exactly as you treat them. You can see the speck in your friend's eye, but you don't notice the log in your own eye.

Matthew 7:1–3 CEV

*Y*ears ago, a Louisiana representative fought to pass a drunk-driving law that would result in the offender serving a mandatory prison sentence. It was a major victory to every advocate against drinking and driving. Shortly after the bill became law, the first offender was arrested for driving under the influence. He was brought to court where the judge found him guilty and sentenced him to prison. Who was the first offender? The legislator who fought to pass the law!

In recent years we've read or heard similar stories. Sadly, the pastor who preaches adamantly against homosexuality and infidelity had committed the same indiscretions he had stood against.

Closer to home, have you ever opposed gossiping, yet gossiped yourself?

Do you teach your kids to tell the truth but then lie to them? Has a friend's preoccupation with herself unnerved you, only to later find yourself doing the same thing?

Jesus addressed the irony of casting judgment. We notice the "speck" in someone's eye as if we're carrying a magnifying glass. "I just don't understand her," we say as we faultfind over the smallest indiscretions. Yet we rationalize or underplay our own faults, the virtual plank in our own eyes.

The Christian woman who rarely notices the speck in another's eye is the woman of God who's too busy working her own sawmill.

You're Equipped!

"I have singled him {Abraham} out so that he will direct his sons and their families to keep the way of the LORD by doing what is right and just. Then I will do for Abraham all that I have promised."

GENESIS 18:19 NLT

*D*o you consider yourself a leader? You might think: *No way!* Yet if you're a mom or you have anyone who is under your care or direction in any capacity, you are indeed a leader!

What you say, think, and do is noteworthy because God placed you in that position. Parents have the responsibility to lead their families to "keep the way of the LORD by doing what is right and just." About now, you might argue: "Great! Like I don't have enough parental responsibilities?" But God has singled us out to direct our children and others to do what's right and fair.

But how can we direct others when we are in need

of direction ourselves? We all need help and support. Our churches and our friends, but most of all our God, give us the support we need to equip us for the job of caring for others and leading them to the Lord.

God never calls us to a task without equipping us to perform the job. In other words, you're not alone. The Holy Spirit gives you not only the strength but the words to lead your children on the right path. He opens opportunities for you to share your faith with others or instruct them to do what is right in God's sight.

God encourages, saying, "Lead them, and I'll lead you. Bless them, and I'll bless you. Care for them, and I'll care for you. Uphold them, and I'll uphold you. Be just and right, and my righteousness and justice will reward you." So lead on!

Right or Wrong?

*Why can't you decide for
yourselves what is right?*

LUKE 12:57 NLT

*H*ave you ever heard, "You should know better"?
Jesus said the same to His followers. They heard Him
preach; they absorbed His teachings; they witnessed
His miracles; they knew Him. And yet they just didn't
get it.

So Jesus told them, "Listen, you know the
signs of an upcoming storm or a scorching day. You
interpret the sky, but you refuse to notice what's right
or wrong!"

Isaiah 5:20 warns us about calling evil good
and good evil. Yet that's exactly what has happened
in today's world. What was once offensive and
unacceptable is now not only acceptable but
applauded. Some folks have lost the will or courage
to call sin sin, and in not doing so, they can no longer

discern what's right or wrong.

A child knows when he or she is wrong without as much as a hint. It's built in. We call it our conscience. When our child snatches a cookie before dinner, he's aware of what he's doing. If our daughter lies, she instantly knows it. But should a person continue to lack discernment of good and evil, they will eventually become confused, unable to determine what is right anymore.

Someone once said: "We need to go back to the way it was thirty years ago, when everybody had Grandma and Grandpa and we were willing to pass moral judgments about right and wrong."

Christian women don't need grandparents or parents to help them distinguish right from wrong. We have the Lord, and He's ever present to give us the wisdom and discernment we all need, whenever and wherever we need it.

Look Up

O LORD, bear my plea for justice.
Listen to my cry for help. Pay attention to
my prayer, for it comes from honest lips.

PSALM 17:1 NLT

When we're flat on our backs, the only way to look is up. That's not a bad thing.

Paige was frustrated and tormented. She loved the Lord and followed Him faithfully, yet one problem after another bombarded her faith and affected her life. She began to wonder if God dismissed her prayers or if she had done something wrong that prevented her from receiving the peace, healing, and direction she sought. *Did God abandon me?* she wondered.

When she finally thought things couldn't get any worse, another woman spread false rumors about her. Shaken, hurt, and at the end of her rope, she cried out to God, just as David did in the above verse. All she wanted was justice; she pleaded for God to make things right again.

Have you ever felt that way? Many of us have faced similar situations that have flattened our faith, crushed our optimism, and demolished our joy. We wonder if our lives will ever be the same again. Often, they aren't. But one thing is sure: God will never forsake or fail us.

Flat on our backs, we cry out to God, voicing exactly how we feel. (After all, He knows anyway.) But He desires for us to turn to Him—not to try by our own strength, which fails, or to turn to others, who sometimes don't understand. But go straight to the Master. That's what David did, and we must follow his lead. When we do, we can rest assured that God will not only answer but change us for the better in the process.

We live in an unfair world, but we serve a just God. He'll make it right. Just ask Him.

Can I Live a Righteous Life?

It was to demonstrate and prove at the present time (in the now season) that He Himself is righteous and that He justifies and accepts as righteous him who has {true} faith in Jesus.

ROMANS 3:26 AMP

By just thinking and doing the right things, do we get to heaven? After all, plenty of people who profess little or no faith perform good deeds and live uprightly.

In Romans, Paul gives the early church the answer. We can't save ourselves through good works. Church attendance doesn't save us either. We're all sinners. In fact, the Bible says: "There is none righteous, no, not one" (Romans 3:10 KJV). We can't perform enough good deeds or attend enough church services to "qualify" for heaven.

Only one person who walked this earth was perfect: Jesus Christ. He was God who left His heavenly throne to walk among us, yet He never sinned. Because He never sinned, He became the perfect sacrifice for all of humankind. . .all sinners, then and now.

The above verse notes that Jesus' righteousness justifies or vindicates us. It's as if we stand guilty before a just judge, and the judge, due to our transgressions, must declare punishment for our sins ("the wages of sin is death"). But after our sentencing he removes his governing robe, descends the platform, and stands alongside of us and says, "Now I will take the punishment on your behalf."

That's exactly what Christ did through the cross. He died so that we might live eternally in heaven. He provided the gift of salvation through Jesus Christ. All we need do is accept that gift into our hearts and lives. Then God sees us through the mirror of His own image, and we are righteous in His sight.

It's always right to do right, but it must begin with repenting of our sins and accepting God's forgiveness. That is the ultimate right thing to do!

God would not rub so hard if it were not to fetch out the dirt that is ingrained in our natures. God loves purity so well He had rather see a hole than a spot in His child's garments.

WILLIAM GURNALL

Purity:
The Christian's Holy Grail

> *Blessed are the pure in heart:*
> *for they shall see God.*
> MATTHEW 5:8 KJV

What composes a pure heart? How do we get one? Jesus assembled His disciples for the Sermon on the Mount and taught them the Beatitudes—a revelation of God's principles of righteousness and holiness.

The sixth beatitude, "Blessed are the pure in heart," pertains to those whom God has delivered from sin's stronghold through His grace and forgiveness. It is the Christian's holy grail.

Purity of heart, however, is only attained through Christ, who empowers us to acquire it. On our own, we can achieve only some changes. For example, Libby once loved to prank people, until she realized that her jokes were hurtful. So she had a change of heart and stopped. That's honorable, but purity of heart is something more.

The pure in heart strive to align with God's holy law, His nature, and His will.

One who is pure in heart desires the very heart of God! She detests evil and embraces righteousness. She desires God's desires above her own.

The Bible tells us that the heart is the wellspring of life (Proverbs 4:23). It's the core of our thoughts, emotions, character, and intellect. Apart from God, the heart is "deceitfully wicked," but the renewed heart through Christ is a wellspring of life.

Do you need a change of heart? That change is just a prayer away. Ask Jesus to come into your heart and forgive you of your sins right now, and He will do the rest. No need to strive and strain for a pure heart. God does the changing.

Win Them
without a Word

*Wives, in the same way submit yourselves to
your own husbands so that, if any of them do not
believe the word, they may be won over without
words by the behavior of their wives, when they
see the purity and reverence of your lives.
Your beauty should not come from
outward adornment.*

1 PETER 3:1–3 NIV

Laurie, a new Christian, prayed for her husband daily.
In an attempt to reach him for Christ she placed Bible
tracts on the back of the toilet, hoping he'd read one,
and she quoted scriptures to him often. She repeatedly
invited him to church, and the more she nagged, the
more he resisted. Arguments ensued, and she'd end up
running to her bedroom in tears. "What's the answer,
Lord? How can I reach him?" she'd plead.

While her husband was at work, Laurie kept a
prayer list because she'd often pray with her friend

over the phone during the day. One day her husband returned home early and discovered the list. His name topped it. In a rampage, he screamed at her so loudly that her Christian neighbor heard the rant and called another believer to pray for Laurie.

Disheartened and hurt, Laurie cried out to God saying, "That's it! I've had it, Lord! He's *Your* problem. I'm done praying for him!" Silently the Lord spoke to her heart: *"Don't preach; just love him."* Obedient, Laurie followed God's command, and three months later her husband accepted Christ.

Unsaved loved ones are saved through our examples of purity and love, not our words. Our behavior is what touches their lives with God's grace. Are we poor examples of godliness? Do we push, nag, or preach? When we do, we alienate them from ourselves and God. But when we accept and love them from a pure heart as God loves and accepts us, they will notice and desire what we have. That's authentic beauty.

Pride and Purity?

*There is a class of people who are pure
in their own eyes, and yet are not
washed from their own filth.*

PROVERBS 30:12 AMP

Uh-oh. Know any people who think a little too
much of themselves? The above passage says it like it
is–refusing to acknowledge our imperfections doesn't
make them go away.

Pride and purity go together like oil and water.
They don't mix. If we think we're pure yet live an
ungodly, impure, sinful life, we're self-deceived.
Purity is more than abstaining from impure behavior.
It involves our thoughts, feelings, and conversations
as well.

Natalie prided herself in good works. She
volunteered at the hospital, supported the
local YMCA, and donated items to charitable
organizations. If someone asked her a favor, she

readily agreed. She believed she was living a pure life even though she often fantasized about other men, bragged about her appearance and lifestyle, and gossiped frequently. Lying and her predisposition to anger were normal behavior. "After all," she rationalized, "I'm only human; what's the big deal?"

C. S. Lewis said: "The moment good taste knows itself, some of its goodness is lost." That's what happens when we think too highly of ourselves. We miss what God wants to teach us, and we stunt our spiritual growth. On the other hand, when we realize we are impure human beings in need of salvation, inner cleansing, and forgiveness, purity emerges like a dormant tulip in the spring. And pride is pulverized!

Pure Thoughts and No Nesting

Everything is pure for someone whose heart is pure. But nothing is pure for an unbeliever with a dirty mind. That person's mind and conscience are destroyed.

TITUS 4:15 CEV

I don't get it, Phyllis thought after a coworker told a dirty joke to a group of fellow employees. Phyllis sincerely missed the punch line because her mind just didn't think that way.

Phyllis had walked with the Lord for many years. Her thoughts were established, rooted, and grounded in His Word. That didn't mean she never sinned or that a bad thought never entered her mind, but she rejected it. Her thoughts aligned with whatever was pure rather than whatever was ugly, nasty, or dirty.

No one is exempt from bad thoughts. That's a given living in this sinful world. But as some say: "It's one thing for a bird to fly over your head; it's another thing for it to nest there." Bad or negative thoughts will come; what we do with them is the real test of our faith. Do we give place to impure thoughts? If so, the bird is starting to nest!

The woman who refuses to allow ungodly thoughts to linger is the woman whose heart is pure. She wants to please God and grow in Him. She longs to live for Christ in thought, word, and deed.

That's what Phyllis did. Her thoughts were void of gutter thinking because, although the bird flew overhead, she refused it residency. Yet the moment we surrender to evil thoughts and allow the bird to nest, we open the door to Satan as our first houseguest.

But for those who are pure, there's no need for concern. The bird just keeps on flying.

Living Examples of Light

> *You will be the pure and innocent children of God. You live among people who are crooked and evil, but you must not do anything that they can say is wrong. Try to shine as lights among the people of this world.*
>
> PHILIPPIANS 2:15 CEV

How important is living a pure life? From his prison cell, Paul instructed and encouraged the Philippian believers to live exemplary lives in a corrupt world. The world was crooked and evil then, and one need only pick up a newspaper or click the remote or computer mouse to know this is even truer today.

Sadly, corruption has infiltrated the Church as well. What was once unacceptable to Christians is now watered down to suit politically correct thinking and behavior. We excuse the once inexcusable; we turn a deaf ear to the once offensive language; we gently dabble in behavior that Christians once rejected.

Holiness is rarely talked about or preached from our pulpits. Gradually, even God's own have justified the ways of the world–so much so that it is often difficult to distinguish a Christian from a non-Christian.

So Paul makes it clear: to know Christ is to walk in purity and innocence. True believers aren't naive, but we are blameless.

Do others know you're a Christian? Is there something good and pure about you that others notice? Or do you act and talk just like the world does?

If the unbeliever witnesses us lying, cheating, gossiping, and doing what others in the world do, why would they want what we have?

The world is filled with darkness, but Jesus is the Light of the World. We are His lamps, living sources of illumination casting beams of forgiveness, love, and purity wherever we go to whomever we meet. So shine on, ladies!

Are You Armed for Battle?

How can a young person stay on the path of purity? By living according to your word.

PSALM 119:9 NIV

From television commercials to movie theaters, sexual connotations thrive. So how do we and our children remain pure? Some parents have removed television, disallowed Facebook forums, and monitored computer activity in their homes. Not a bad idea. Yet there will always be another avenue through which the enemy of our souls will attempt to reach us with impure thoughts.

Did you ever accidently see something that you couldn't get out of your mind? No matter how hard you tried, that awful image branded your brain. Have you ever watched a movie with sexual scenes that stayed with you? Did you do something in your youth that you regret now but can't overcome? The scriptures instruct us to guard our thoughts and protect what we allow into our spirits.

So how do we combat impure thoughts or lifestyles? God always makes a way. Paul said in his letter to the Ephesians, "Put on the whole armour of God, that ye may be able to stand against the wiles of the devil" (Ephesians 6:44 KJV).

The Holy Spirit equips us with the "sword of the Spirit," God's Word. The more we consume the meat of God's Word, the more it becomes a part of us. As we meditate on the scriptures, our minds produce good, pure, and honest thinking. We are equipped to banish impure thoughts and actions as we advance forward fully geared for spiritual battle. So put on God's armor and walk boldly. You're equipped!

The Refiner

*Fire tests the purity of silver and gold,
but the LORD tests the heart.*

PROVERBS 17:3 NLT

A refiner sat patiently alongside a fiery pot filled
with precious metals. The purification process was
necessary to remove all of the metals' impurities. The
aged refiner watched the process intently as a woman
passed by. Curious, she asked, "Must you watch the
silver every moment?" The man replied, "Oh yes, if
left in the flame too long, the fire will damage the
silver, so I wait until it has been in just long enough."
As the dross skimmed to the top, the woman probed
further. "How do you know when the metal is ready?"
With a gentle smile the refiner said, "I know it is
ready when I can see my reflection in it."

Malachi 3:3 (KJV) says, "And he {God} shall sit
as a refiner and purifier of silver." God allows fiery
trials for a reason. Without problems, we wouldn't

pray as much as we do. Without trials, how would we experience God's power, grace, and mercy?

From glory to glory God is changing you. Are you going through a rough time?

Do you feel God has abandoned you? Are you bombarded with negative thoughts about your future or the future of a loved one? What you are experiencing is what every true believer goes through–the refining process of purification in the heart and mind. We have dross–the excess, needless thoughts and attitudes–that needs skimming before we can become the person God intends.

You are God's own–His precious silver. Don't worry, the fire won't destroy you; instead, God waits patiently until He sees in you His own reflection.

Obedience: The Key to God's Blessings

Oh, that you had hearkened to My commandments! Then your peace and prosperity would have been like a flowing river, and your righteousness {the holiness and purity of the nation} like the {abundant} waves of the sea.

ISAIAH 48:18 AMP

*W*hy can't you just do what I tell you?" we ask our kids in frustration. "Why can't you just *listen* for once?" Every mom has experienced this type of aggravation. If your son had only remembered to put his basketball uniform in his duffel bag like you kept telling him, he would not have had to sit out the game. And didn't you ask your daughter repeatedly to please remove some of her shoes from the mudroom before someone tripped on them? She didn't, and your elderly mom caught her walker in one of the shoes and nearly fell. Disciplinary measures were in order.

God has experienced parental frustrations with

His kids, too. He told the Israelites that if they had only listened to His commands, they would have enjoyed peace, prosperity, holiness, and purity as an entire nation! Obviously, they didn't obey and suffered the consequences.

That scripture holds true for believers today, too. How many times could we have avoided a problem if we had only listened to the Spirit's still, small voice and obeyed? It's not that God waits for us to mess up so He can punish us, but He does allow us to reap the consequences of our disobedience. He allows us to go our own way until we meet with disaster and surrender to Him and His will for our lives.

Oswald Chambers wrote: "The agony of man's affliction is often necessary to put him into the right mood to face the fundamental things of life. The psalmist said, 'Before I was afflicted I went astray; but now I have kept Thy Word.' "

What's the key to the blessings of holiness, purity, prosperity, and peace? Obedience. Now if we could only drive home that point to our kids!

Teach me your ways, O LORD, that I may live
according to your truth! Grant me purity of
heart, so that I may honor you.

PSALM 86:11 NLT

Have you ever conversed over coffee with someone about a common interest? Perhaps she was an accomplished pianist or artist, and you wanted to pick her brain to learn all you could about her particular area of expertise. This was your golden opportunity to learn more than you could ever find in a classroom.

That's how we should approach God. Open. Eager. We desire to learn His ways so that we can become more like Him and honor Him with our lives.

The psalmist David sinned, yet he was a man after God's own heart. Today, God still seeks men and women after His heart–after His pure heart. That's why the psalmist prayed, "Teach me your ways, O LORD!" His desire came from a humble, contrite heart eager to learn.

Purity of heart is the vessel—the holy grail—that houses all other godly characteristics, thoughts, intents, feelings, and emotions of a believer determined to become and do what God has always intended for her.

Purity of heart says, "I desire my way, nevertheless not my will, but Your will be done." It announces, "I am not my own; I was bought with a price paid for me on Calvary." It proclaims, "Jesus is Lord, and I will follow Him despite what others choose to do."

The pure in heart seek justice and mercy; they are peacemakers and lovers of God and anything good and honest. They are patient, understanding, and they listen with kindness, not judgment. They are women after God's own heart.

Out of all things lovely, God transcends them all. His magnificence and beauty are reflected in a pristine landscape and in the countenance of a transformed sinner. Who but the Savior possesses and provides the capacity to love and forgive the ugliest among us?

TINA KRAUSE

How Lovely

God's Presence: How Lovely

How lovely is your dwelling place,
Lord Almighty!
Psalm 84:1 niv

*Y*ou walk into a friend's house, and from the moment you step across the threshold you're at home. With a warm welcome, perhaps an embrace or smile, your host invites you to sit down. "Would you like a cup of tea?" she inquires, as you nestle into a comfy chair next to a cozy fire. "Sure," you reply, absorbing the atmosphere and the peace that swaddles you like a warm blanket. *How lovely*, you ponder as you breathe deep and relax, conversing with a friend heart-to-heart.

You've needed this quiet time with a friend, apart from your upside-down world. In her home you've found rest. It's not so much the home's decor, albeit it's homey and inviting, but the loving person with whom you are spending time that makes this moment special.

In Psalms, David exhibited similar expressions of contentment and peace. God's dwelling place is lovely. How lovely it is to spend time with the Lord. He is a respite from life's chaos; His presence instantly hugs us with peace, calmness, and security.

To take time apart from our world and enter into God's presence is like snuggling in a comfy chair next to a warm fire on a frigid day. "Can I help you?" the Savior inquires. We volley a snappy response. "Oh, Lord! I need You; I need Your peace, direction, and rest." Suddenly we're immersed in the quietness of His gentle love and care as He speaks to us the way only He can. We converse as close friends do, and we find pleasure in our surroundings, just the two of us sharing heart-to-heart.

Timely advice is lovely,
like golden apples in a silver basket.

PROVERBS 25:44 NLT

What do you consider lovely? A beautiful, well-arranged bouquet of flowers? A million-dollar view? A breathtaking sunset? Or how about that flattering, slimming dress? Often, the scriptures used the word "lovely" to describe beautiful women like Esther, Rachel, Sarah, and Job's daughters. They were lovely "in figure and form."

But the scriptures underscore godly attributes and characteristics as more lovely than the most stunning women. Attributes like timely advice. If you've ever experienced receiving just the right advice at just the right time, you understand.

Maybe you've sought counsel about a personal problem, and although everyone has an opinion, their words are barren. You know that they mean well, but their advice just doesn't strike a chord. You seek God, confide in friends, and still nothing. Just about the time your back is against the wall, someone or something happens to deliver the words that click. Your problem makes sense for the first time, and you're able to move forward in confidence. How lovely!

Imagine a shiny silver basket brimming with plump, perfect golden apples. How gorgeous to look at. In fact, you wish you had an arrangement for your dining room table, just to add to the beauty of your home. That's the kind of pleasure we find in sound, godly advice given at the very moment we need it most.

Timely advice is a treasure. Need some today? Rest assured, God will deliver, and it will come right on time.

*As it is written: "How beautiful are
the feet of those who bring good news!"*

Romans 10:15 niv

Society's description of genuine loveliness is not
God's version. A few definitions of lovely are
"beautiful, pleasing especially in a harmonious way,
delightful, caring, and loving." And yes, lovely also
means "stunning in appearance."

We've all met or know of women who are
genuinely beautiful outside but horribly ugly inside.
As the saying goes, outward beauty fades. But God
interprets true loveliness and beauty as the individual
with a heart in harmony with His own.

The apostle Paul reminded the Roman believers
what God thought about those who devoted their
lives to bringing the Gospel to others. They're
beautiful! Their feet move them from one place to
another spreading God's Word. Paul emphasized the

importance of preaching the Gospel, saying, "How, then, can they call on the one they have not believed in? And how can they believe in the one of whom they have not heard?" (Romans 10:14 NIV). He went on to exhort them to share the Word, because if unbelievers don't hear, they can't receive.

The truth is, not just pastors or evangelists are called to share the Gospel; we all are. We all have a circle of friends, acquaintances, or coworkers. We live in a world filled with people who don't know Christ. And, in some cases, we will be the only Bible they'll ever read.

So what stops us? Rejection? The fear of standing apart from the crowd? We don't want others to dub us a religious fanatic, so we remain silent.

When we discover a great find or we hear about a great sale, don't we share it with our friends? How much more should we share the good news of the living Christ and eternal salvation?

After all, those lovely feet of yours were made for talking in your walk with the Lord.

Jesus: Our Best Friend

Now Jesus loved Martha and her sister
and Lazarus. {They were His dear friends,
and He held them in loving esteem.}

JOHN 11:5 AMP

*W*hat do you suppose Martha, Mary, and Lazarus
did that made the King of kings hold them in such
high regard and loving esteem? Were they more
special than anyone else? What characteristics or
acts of kindness caused Jesus to feel at home in their
residence? Surely His feelings toward them had to
originate beyond their hospitality, although they were
genuinely hospitable.

Imagine John recording that Jesus called you His
friend, holding you in loving esteem. Wow! That's far
better than the president of the United States holding
a press conference to announce that you were among
three of his closest, most trusted, highly honored
friends! Instantly, press crews would converge upon

your home, bombarding you with questions. What did you do to gain such notoriety? How did you become so close? What's the president really like?

God Himself loved this trio of dear friends. They were lovely and lovable in His sight, despite their personal flaws. Lazarus and his two sisters, Martha and Mary, lived in Bethany, where Jesus and His disciples often found rest from their ministry. Martha was a type-A personality, while Mary was more demur. Martha ran the household, preparing and serving meals, while Mary enjoyed sitting at Jesus' feet to absorb His teachings. When Martha scolded her sister and asked Jesus to make her come and help, Jesus responded: "My dear Martha, you are worried and upset over all these details! There is only one thing worth being concerned about. Mary has discovered it" (Luke 10:38–42 NLT).

Yet Jesus loved Martha as much as He loved her brother Lazarus (whom He later raised from the dead) and teachable Mary.

No matter our differing personalities, God calls us His friends, too, when we invite Him into our hearts and homes. We'll never find another friend like Him. Does Jesus feel at home in your heart?

His Loveliness Uplifts

Praise the LORD, for the LORD is good;
celebrate his lovely name with music.

PSALM 135:3 NLT

*Y*ou're down. It's been an awful week. Everything that could go wrong did, and you'd love to escape to somewhere void of problems and hassles–just for a day. Even for a moment!

You dress for church and enter the sanctuary, greeting some friends and acquaintances along the way. *Time to put on a smile, no matter how I feel*, you think. Then the music starts. At first, you reluctantly join in. But before long, you begin to immerse yourself in praise. The music and lyrics lift your burdens as you focus on Jesus rather than yourself. Joy comes, perhaps for the first time all week, or in weeks! What a relief! What a pleasure as you, together with other believers, celebrate the Lord with music.

Good music produces a positive heart and frame

of mind. Maybe that's why King David loved music so much. He was a poet and musician and expressed his feelings, thoughts, and love for God through his lyrics and instruments. The book of Psalms overflows with his compositions.

As Christians, we often turn to Psalms for comfort or relief, just as we turn to Christian praise music to elevate us beyond our earthly trials, if only for a few moments.

God gives us a reprieve when we sing His praises. He alone is lovely, and His loveliness pours into our barren lives just when we need it. So sing! He is "altogether lovely."

God's Opposites Attract?
Or Divide?

*Keep on loving one another
as brothers and sisters.*

HEBREWS 13:1 NIV

"How do you like my two new suits?" Judy's husband proudly inquired after returning from the store. "See the pinstripes?"

"Uh, sure," she replied, grabbing a magnifying glass for closer examination. "I see you went all out with that tiny splash of color!"

"Yeah, nice huh?" her husband responded.

"Sure, Jim, but which suit is navy and which one is black?"

Judy and her husband are complete opposites. She loves vibrant colors or creamy pastels; he loves muted gray, black, and navy tones. Judy gravitates toward the latest trends, while Jim sticks to traditional or classical designs.

Yet neither is wrong. They discovered early on that, although opposite, together they complement each other.

The Body of Christ is similar. We all have our different forms of worship and attend different churches. Yet we all belong to God despite our differences and preferences.

The Bible repeatedly instructs us to love one another. Jesus prayed, saying, "Father, protect them by the power of your name, the name you gave me, so that they may be one as we are one" (John 17:11 NIV). Too often we focus on our differences and judge one another. But "God prizes Christian unity above doctrinal exactitude."

After all, it is not *where* we worship but *whom* we worship. Denominational differences will mean little when we view the face of Jesus. Quibbling over the style and color of our spiritual clothes is foolish in the kingdom of God. Knowing the Master Tailor is what really counts. In the end, loving others is what God desires of us.

Characteristics
of the Lovely

*But he must be hospitable (loving and a friend
to believers, especially to strangers and
foreigners); {he must be} a lover of goodness
{of good people and good things}, sober-minded
(sensible, discreet), upright and fair-minded,
a devout man and religiously correct, temperate
and keeping himself in hand.*

TITUS 1:8 AMP

*W*ow, what a grand house!" "Her gown is exquisite!"
"His work ethic is top-notch!" "She is lovely in every
way." "Her sound reputation is unsurpassed." These
comments define loveliness as being lovable, grand,
exquisite, top-notch, unsurpassed, first-class, or
attractive.

In the above passage, Titus outlined the
characteristics of a leader. Those attributes are, in two
words, *lovely* and *lovable*. They are the hallmarks and
qualities of our loving God, and those who strive to

achieve them must do so with a teachable, humble, dedicated heart to service.

So for the fun of it, let's take a quiz. Only you know the answers, of course.

First, are you hospitable? Not only opening your home but your heart to others. Do you welcome in new friends or those foreign to your way of thinking and lifestyle? Do you love the unlovable?

Next, do you sincerely applaud the efforts of a friend or acquaintance who is complimented or credited for her acts of goodness?

Are you sensible and discreet in all of your dealings with others? Do you keep a cool head while others fly off the handle?

Finally, are you upright, fair, a devout believer, and one who holds on to the reins of a flyaway tongue?

Admittedly, we are human and don't fit all of these characteristics all of the time. But Titus gives us attributes to aim for to help us ace the test.

Isn't She Lovely?

Saul and Jonathan were lovely and pleasant in their lives, and in their death they were not divided: they were swifter than eagles, they were stronger than lions.

2 Samuel 1:23 KJV

Don't you enjoy the company of someone who is unselfish and sensitive to others? She's a woman who focuses on how her words or actions affect someone else. She cultivates solid relationships and is a loyal friend, unafraid to defend you.

The Bible records that Saul was Jonathan's dad. Like any father-son relationship, they had their share of disputes and strain. Yet they shared a genuine closeness. Some commentaries suggest that Jonathan raised his son, Mephibosheth, in Saul's house, which means as an adult Jonathan lived with his father for some period of time. The above scripture says that in battle they died together.

Jonathan was a man of courage. He faced danger and death for the sake of his country. Yet his most notable characteristic was his ardent and unselfish devotion to his friends, especially King David. For David, Jonathan relinquished hope for his father's throne and died for those he loved.

A lovely woman of God carries similar traits, like a statuesque vision of integrity and inner beauty. She's royalty in God's eyes, despite her lowly status, unimpressive résumé, or average appearance. She's approachable, honest, faithful, and dependable.

Whenever we think of whatever is lovely, we think of people whose lives so positively influence, embrace, and love others that we anticipate spending time with them. That's every Christian woman's hope: to become God's vision of true loveliness.

God's Loving Eye Is on You

*I will instruct you and teach you in
the way you should go; I will counsel
you with my loving eye on you.*

PSALM 32:8 NIV

*E*very mom or grandma has witnessed her children
at play. The toddler who fumbles to place one block
atop another; the little princess who places her stuffed
animals in chairs at a table set with plastic cups and
saucers ready for tea; the little boy who jumps for joy,
arms outstretched, after he catches the baseball for the
very first time. Priceless moments.

We lovingly watch them with smiles as occa-
sional giggles erupt despite our hand over our
mouth. Throughout their lives we lovingly observe
their endeavors, from first steps to first dates. We
applaud their accomplishments and take pride in
their efforts. We discipline and sometimes experience
disappointment. First we hold them as infants, then

we mold them as children, until we finally let go and pray that they will become all God intended.

That's what God does. Our heavenly Father keeps "a loving eye" on us. He helps us with first steps and major hurdles. He holds, molds, and lets go at just the right stages of our spiritual lives, even when we don't deserve His love.

Renowned preacher Charles H. Spurgeon told this story: "Once, while riding in the country, I saw a farmer's barn weather vane on the arrow of which was inscribed these words: 'God is Love.' I turned in at the gate and asked the farmer, 'What do you mean by that? Do you think God's love is changeable; that it veers about as that arrow turns in the winds?' The farmer replied, 'Oh no! I mean that whichever way the wind blows, God is still love.' "

The Highest
Form of Love

*Our great desire is that you will keep
on loving others as long as life lasts.*

HEBREWS 6:11 NLT

What is love of the highest kind? A mother's love?
The love of a devoted and loving husband? How about
the very love of God extended to another–and not just
anyone–the one who deserves God's love the least?

T. E. McCully was the father of Ed McCully, one
of several missionaries killed by the Auca Indians in
Ecuador. Imagine the horror of losing your child at
the hand of a killer. The loss of a child–despite his or
her age–would be dreadful enough, but if our innocent
offspring was slain at the hand of a murderer he was
trying to help, our anger, angst, horror, and bitterness
would be incomprehensible to most. What's more,
what if the only reason for his death was due to your
son's love for God and for the very people who killed
him?

But T. E. McCully didn't raise his fist to the heavens or think of ways to retaliate. He expressed no hatred or rage. No one would blame him if he did. Instead, the grieving father prayed, saying, "Lord, let me live long enough to see those fellows saved who killed our boys that I may throw my arms around them and tell them I love them because they love my Christ."

The world tosses around the word "love" without realizing the true meaning of it.

God's love is an unconditional, agape love. Mature Christians exhibit that kind of love to the ugliest, most detestable, most unlovable, and most unlikely individuals, as Christ empowers them with the highest form of love—His own.

It's easy to love the lovable. But few of us choose the capacity to love those so vile, so unworthy, so deplorable as the men who killed those missionaries. Yet that's what God did and does for us. Jesus died for every sinner. He took the unworthy, even the most heinous, and transformed us with the message of salvation through Jesus Christ.

There is no greater love.

{ *It takes many good deeds
to build a good reputation,
and only one bad one to lose it.*

BENJAMIN FRANKLIN }

A Good Report Equals
a Good Reputation

What a Reputation!

A good name is better than precious ointment.
ECCLESIASTES 7:1 KJV

*Y*our child receives a good report card. Your boss gives you a glowing assessment. People speak highly of you. Your enemies respect you. Reputation. Everyone has one, whether good, bad, or in between.

There are some actions that are universally commendable such as courtesy, kindness, respect for authority, purity, a solid work ethic, dependability, trustworthiness, and integrity. Anyone who exhibits these virtues is commendable; they not only possess noteworthy characteristics but demonstrate them through their thoughts, words, and deeds. Their lives are a "good report," as Philippians 4:8 states.

We are to concentrate on whatever is admirable. And our reputations are of utmost importance. Dwight L. Moody said, "If I take care of my character, my reputation will take care of me."

Women of strong character need not worry about how they appear to others. We needn't hope to make a good, lasting impression or strive for the favor of others. Godly characteristics automatically translate into a good reputation. Like a precious ointment, a good name will exude everything that is commendable, of good report.

In a world saturated with bad news, evil deeds, horrific acts of violence, and sexual impurities, God allows His children to beam the light of His Word through an unsurpassed, indisputable reputation based on His power and our love for Him. Ah, how soothing those precious ointments are.

Reputation or Riches?

Choose a good reputation over great riches;
being held in high esteem is better
than silver or gold.

PROVERBS 22:1 NLT

Remember high school? Although some of us can't even remember what we had for lunch, most of our high school days linger. High school exalted the pretty elite–those girls whose beauty won them the boys' attention and popularity of the class. Cliques were expected, and whatever group you were in was the type of girl you were labeled as. What most of us discovered was that popularity didn't necessarily equal good reputation. Some classmates, although pretty, were snobby and mean. They garnered the attention of others, and some of them gloated with pride.

As Christian women, we put immaturity behind us. We know that a good reputation doesn't come from what fashions we wear, who we know, how big our houses are, or how beautiful we are, but through our inner character.

The scripture says that a good reputation is more valuable than great wealth. For others to think of us with the highest esteem and respect is a precious commodity. You can't buy a good reputation; you earn it.

Henry Ford noted: "You cannot build a reputation on what you are going to do."

In other words, thinking about it alone doesn't make it happen. A solid reputation is built on good character. Thinking about helping someone isn't helpful until you act on that thought. Women of character don't strive to produce these attributes any more than fruit strains to mature on the tree. With time, wisdom, experience, and obedience to God's Word, character is formed, and a good reputation occurs as a result. That's rich!

As the World Watches

Furthermore, he must have a good reputation and be well thought of by those outside {the church}, lest he become involved in slander and incur reproach and fall into the devil's trap.

1 TIMOTHY 3:7 AMP

Life oozes with petty annoyances and problems. At times, maintaining our good witness is a chore. Your neighbor allows his dog to bark incessantly, even after you've asked him to please do something about it. Your coworker thinks she knows it all and offers you unsolicited advice, talking down to you even though you have seniority. An acquaintance has targeted you with false accusations, and you're clueless. A self-absorbed family member calls you daily with "favors" to ask, knowing full well that your schedule is already past full. These irritations turn into major issues only when we let them. You'd love to give these folks a piece of your mind. But you resist the temptation and handle it with a kind approach to the problem. Why? Because God instructs us to resort to honorable behavior even when we are dishonored, berated, or misunderstood.

The fact is, no matter how cordial and courteous we are, the world watches intently, waiting to find fault with us. First Timothy instructs the Church to maintain a good reputation in the world despite the people who are eager to dissect our every word or accuse us of a dishonorable act.

Godly women live in such a way that unbelievers notice that our faith in Christ is real. Maintaining a sound reputation means holding our tongues, though we want to lash out. Although it's hard to subdue our anger when we're falsely accused or mistreated, if we handle these situations in a direct yet loving manner, God is glorified.

We can disarm these people with a gentle approach. Do you struggle with an uncooperative neighbor? An irritating coworker? An annoying relative? Fight back with kindness and a good reputation.

Does Your Reputation Precede You?

Paul came. . .to Lystra, where a disciple named Timothy lived, whose mother was Jewish and a believer but whose father was a Greek.
The believers at Lystra and Iconium spoke well of him. Paul wanted to take him along on the journey.
ACTS 16:1–3 NIV

*H*ey, I've heard about you!" Anita said in excitement after she met an older woman of whom others spoke highly.

Anita's statement stunned the woman. "Uh-oh, what did you hear?" she joked.

"Everything good," Anita stated.

What a compliment! The woman's reputation preceded her. She was a woman of high esteem and sound moral character. How commendable.

Young Timothy's reputation preceded him, too. So much so that Paul desired for Timothy to join him on his missionary journeys. Although Timothy's mother was a believer who taught him the ways of the Lord, his father was not. Yet the influence she had on him is recorded in the epistles through the life he led for the sake of the Gospel.

Whether or not we have children, spiritual or otherwise, we have a calling. God asks us to influence our children, nieces or nephews, friends, neighbors, and whomever we meet for the kingdom's sake.

Just as Paul chose Timothy because of the glowing reports he heard about him, keeping good company helps us on our journey. George Washington said: "Associate with men of good quality if you esteem your own reputation; for it is better to be alone than in bad company."

Do we demonstrate God's ways? Are our actions and words uplifting, pointing others to Christ? Does our reputation precede us? It's something to ponder.

A Reputation to Serve

*But made himself of no reputation,
and took upon him the form of a servant,
and was made in the likeness of men.*

PHILIPPIANS 2:7 KJV

Jesus in all His glory, power, knowledge, and authority descended to our level to became one of us. He set aside His kingship and he humbled Himself to provide salvation and service.

How unlike us. If we receive accolades, we glow in the recognition; if we gain a promotion we bask in the attention and compliments. Some of us even gloat or brag about our accomplishments. Yet Jesus–the One who deserves all glory, praise, and recognition–debased Himself to serve.

Women of God are called to do the same. What is your area of service? Are you known for your great cooking or baking? Your sense of humor? Your hospitality and eagerness to volunteer? Are you acknowledged for being a good mom, wife, or grandmother? Do others look to you for wisdom or encouragement? All of these traits are reputable, yet above any and all of our gifts and attributes, serving Christ should top the list.

Everyone has spiritual and natural gifts to use for Christ; we just need to recognize them. Kathy loves to decorate and saves items she no longer uses. If a newly divorced, widowed, or single mom needs a much-needed boost, she offers to make over her bedroom or living room. Using existing items and adding a few of her own, Kathy rearranges, paints, and adds special touches to make a lackluster room shine. While working, she often shares the love of Christ with the woman who needs to hear how much God loves her. Kathy possesses a desire to serve others through the gift God has given her.

For those of us who could never stand before a large crowd to share Christ or travel to foreign countries as missionaries, we can serve Christ right where we are. We are all called to share the good news of Jesus within our circle of influence. Whether we do that through baking, a word of encouragement, or redecorating a room, God loves a humble servant's heart.

Respect Women
of Good Reputation

*And she must have a reputation for good
deeds, as one who has brought up children,
who has practiced hospitality to strangers
{of the brotherhood}, washed the feet of the
saints, helped to relieve the distressed,
{and} devoted herself diligently to
doing good in every way.*

1 TIMOTHY 5:10 AMP

*A*ttention widows over sixty! First Timothy 5:10 was
intended for you.

The church in Ephesus had an official list of
widows who were entitled to material support from
the church. In biblical times, the government gave no
pensions or assistance to older women who had no
family to help them. So Timothy listed the attributes
of a woman worthy of financial aid.

If we have known the Lord most of our lives,
by the time we reach our sixties we are scripturally

instructed to be known for our good reputation. Notice the empty nesters in your church. The older women are usually the ones who cook, serve, and clean up after church functions. They love little children and often work in the nursery or teach Sunday school. They are experienced at child rearing and grandchildren spoiling. The church depends on their hospitality; after all, these ladies have hosted most of their lives. They've learned patience and kindness, and they understand how much it means to reach out to someone in need. They are dependable prayer warriors. In a word, they serve. An Irish proverb notes: "The work praises the man {or woman}."

These women of good deeds, faithfulness, wisdom, and reputation deserve respect and assistance in their time of need. Do you know of a woman like that? Let her know she's appreciated. *Are* you a woman like that? Bless your heart. Thank you!

A Reputation
of Nonconformity

Am I now trying to win the approval of human beings, or of God? Or am I trying to please people? If I were still trying to please people, I would not be a servant of Christ.

GALATIANS 1:10 NIV

The crowd exploded with excitement as Jesus rode into the city of Jerusalem. Waving palm branches and laying their garments before Him, they cried, "Hosanna! Blessed is He who comes in the name of the Lord!" But a few days later this same crowd shouted, "Crucify Him!"

How could those onlookers change their opinions and attitudes toward Jesus seemingly overnight? Consider today's world. Sadly, this type of inconsistent behavior is not only possible but probable. Although we hate to admit it, popular opinion has influenced us at one time or another.

Yep, human nature produces crowd pleasers,

teetering on the edge of compromise as we lean toward the consensus of the whole. Mark Twain once noted: "We are discreet sheep; we wait to see how the drove is going and then we go with the drove."

Have you ever guarded your true convictions until you assessed the sentiments of the majority? The strongest among us have been known to buckle under popular opinion. Just put a Chicago Bulls fan in the center of a Lakers cheering section. Though his or her team scores, it's guaranteed you won't see that fan jump up in unrestrained applause.

It takes courage to resist conformity. Peter declared his undying dedication to Jesus and hours later denied him three times. But Paul, a rather gutsy individual, upheld his reputation to proclaim Christ without shame. The true test of Paul's and our dedication to the Lord lies in our conviction to stand for the cause of Christ even when the crowds mock, snicker, and scoff at our beliefs.

Bravo to the believers who are reputed to keep perfect cadence to the beat of God's drum in the workplace, streets, stadiums, and marketplaces of life–those gallant few who continue to wave palm branches and shout "Hosanna!" even when the crowd insists "Crucify Him!"

Are You Listening?

In those days when you pray, I will listen.
JEREMIAH 29:12 NLT

Have you noticed that listening is an art few have mastered? Katy first made this observation at a family gathering. Upon the arrival of each guest, the hostess burst with exchanges of polite gestures and niceties. Phrases such as "How good to see you!" and "How are you?" ensued.

Having undergone some serious health problems, Katy responded with "Ah. . .I'm not doing very well." The hostess, oblivious to Katy's response, replied, "Oh, that's good."

In fairness to the hostess, her preoccupation with making her guests feel welcome had distracted her. So instead of hearing what Katy said, she dispensed a pat reply. When we're immersed in our own thoughts, we often miss the undisclosed pain masked behind the words or expressions of others.

With blunt honesty on the art of listening, the late minister and author Jamie Buckingham confessed: "When listening, I have learned it's best to give an impression of interest. Perhaps it's a holdover from the time I used to rush back to the door of the church after a Sunday morning service to shake hands with parishioners. Smiling, always smiling. And agreeing. But never listening. If someone tried to tell me something, I would give them a big 'God bless you, brother,' all the while pulling him through the door as I shook his hand. It's a trick used by politicians and preachers—both notorious as types of people who never listen."

God listens when we pray, and He answers. And He does so not only with an open ear but with an understanding, attentive heart, even when what we say seems insignificant.

Do you have a reputation for being a good listener? Listening is an art form we, too, can master if we take lessons from the Master, Jesus Christ. Because of His example, there's hope for the rest of us to "go and do likewise."

*A person who plans evil will get
a reputation as a troublemaker.*

PROVERBS 24:8 NLT

Have you ever known someone who brings out the
worst in you? When she interacts with others, trouble
begins. A woman not prone to gossip will, under
a troublemaker's influence, begin to join in on the
gossip session.

By nature we are all predisposed to analyzing
and judging others anyway. In the flesh we just can't
seem to keep our unruly tongues from flapping with
opinions about what other women do or don't do. Yet
when we succumb, we become troublemakers.

If someone constantly bashes a mutual friend,
rest assured she does the same to you behind your
back. That's the essence of troublemaking and a
characteristic of a troublemaker.

Some people bad-mouth others because of

feelings of insecurity or jealousy. Yet what they don't realize is when they do, they also create a reputation for themselves as a gossiper and backbiter.

The scriptures warn: "Others may accuse you of gossip, and you will never regain your good reputation" (Proverbs 25:10 NLT).

But commendable behavior exudes trustworthiness and establishes a good reputation for us as women of integrity. Our goal as Christian women is to become all that God wants us to be at home, work, church, or wherever God places us. If we desire to serve and please God, then we must attempt to keep our carnal natures at bay, surrendering to the control of the Holy Spirit. That's the only way to stay out of trouble!

Finding Favor

Then you will find favor with both God and people, and you will earn a good reputation.

PROVERBS 3:4 NLT

*W*ouldn't it be nice to find favor with people and with our God? This verse reminds us that we can. But how? Solomon gives the answer in verse 3 (NIV): "Let love and faithfulness never leave you; bind them around your neck, write them on the tablet of your heart."

We are to know the Word of God and make it an integral part of our lives. It's like breathing. You don't even know that you're implementing and exhibiting godly behavior. It's just a result of your relationship with Christ and your desire to grow and learn.

This kind of behavior not only pleases God but wins others to Christ through our example. Consider the life of evangelist Billy Graham. His integrity and godliness has placed him in positions of prominence—even presidents have sought his counsel. When the unbeliever respects you for your faith, and other believers esteem you for your values, you have won favor with man and with God.

This is the work of the Holy Spirit in our hearts. As we surrender our wills, diligently seek God's face, and walk humbly before God and others, God rewards us with favor.

The book of Luke tells us that "Jesus grew in wisdom and stature, and in favor with God and man" (2:52 NIV). As we follow His example, we can do the same.

{ *A virtuous woman is God's instrument of divine beauty played to the symphony of a noble character and lasting loveliness.* }

TINA KRAUSE

Virtue:
Our Standard of Excellence

Virtue: The Beauty That Deepens

For His divine power has bestowed upon us all things that {are requisite and suited} to life and godliness, through the {full, personal} knowledge of Him Who called us by and to his own glory and excellence {virtue}.

2 PETER 1:3 AMP

Women tend to desire outward beauty. Admit it; some physical characteristics are most enviable! Maybe you wish you had the lips of Angelina Jolie, or the smile of Anne Hathaway or Julia Roberts (who doesn't?). Perhaps you desire thick, shiny hair, a curvaceous figure, or the beauty of a supermodel. So you trek to the store to comb the cosmetic section for products to plump your lips or enhance your beauty. We've all done it. Or perhaps you admire a public figure whom you hope to emulate intellectually. So you study her demeanor, read her books, and attend her lectures.

But to attain godly virtues is a high priority for the Christian woman–trustworthiness, kindness, patience, honesty, humility, respect, wisdom, integrity, godliness, and maturity are just a few. Virtue is striving for moral excellence; it is the essence of the positive characteristics we exhibit in our everyday lives.

In the above passage, Peter tells the Church that God has empowered us to live a life of godliness through the knowledge of Christ. God *calls* us to become like Him, a reflection of His glory and excellence.

Every believer is called to grow in wisdom and knowledge and allow the Holy Spirit to work in our lives so that we begin to reflect the very essence of our Creator–virtues that produce a beauty unsurpassed by external features and endowments. And contrary to our exteriors, this beauty only intensifies as we mature.

Crown Him with Virtue

A virtuous woman is a crown to her husband: but she that maketh ashamed is as rottenness in his bones.

PROVERBS 12:4 KJV

Have you ever made an unkind public comment, perhaps jokingly, about your husband and then regretted it afterward? Some women say things to or about their husbands in a group setting that they would never say to him in the privacy of their homes.

Proverbs says that a virtuous woman is a "crown" to her husband. What comes to mind when you envision a crown? Your daughter's princess tiara? How about Queen Elizabeth's or Miss America's jeweled crests?

One Greek translation of the word describes a crown as a "token of public honor for nuptial joy," and "an emblem of life and joy." That's a closer definition of this scripture's depiction of a crown.

A virtuous woman compliments, enhances, and illuminates her spouse's life with joy and honor. "How can I do that when my husband acts like a moron and doesn't know the Lord?" some well-meaning women ask.

The verse is pretty straightforward; there are no qualifying factors. In fact, we are especially called to live a virtuous life in the presence of those who are without Christ. William E. Channing noted: "The home is the chief school of human virtues." Who knows us better than our spouses, kids, and family members who live with us? It's easy to exhibit virtuous behavior in church or apart from our surroundings, but what about at home? Home is the training ground we need to develop the virtues we seek.

Ladies take note: virtue is a crown to our husbands; criticism and negativity cause his bones to rot. The choice is ours to make.

Act or React?

*The wicked bluff their way through,
but the virtuous think before they act.*

PROVERBS 24:29 NLT

*Y*our coworker pushed you to your limit. For months you shouldered the brunt of her nasty looks, contemptuous remarks, and accusatory tones. Now you've had it! In a burst of anger you "tell her like it is," and storm away. *She deserved that!* you rationalize as angry thoughts whirl faster than a tornado. "Way to go," another coworker encourages as you return to your desk. But even with solid validation and sweet retribution, something nags at you. *Ugh. I should have handled that differently.*

Some of us act; others react. Most women react; it is part of our nature. But as a familiar quotation says: "Christians aren't perfect; we're just forgiven." It's true. Sometimes we blow it and lose control. We act before we think. Even still, God is there to forgive, teach, heal, and help us.

If you have ever been in a confrontational situation and said the wrong thing at the wrong time, don't fret. Just ask for forgiveness. God loves you, and He understands; but He also instructs us to make peace with our enemies. Often that means approaching the other person with an apology as well. Why? Because, although you were right, you approached the issue in the wrong way.

That kind of heartfelt humility is a lovely virtue. The unbeliever may even arrogantly chide you for your prior remarks. Don't allow that to dissuade you from doing whatever it is God leads you to do. You, after all, are accountable to God, and He will reward you accordingly.

Is Becoming a Virtuous Woman Attainable?

"There are many virtuous and capable women in the world, but you surpass them all!"

PROVERBS 31:29 NLT

*W*ow, what a compliment! Who *is* this woman? Proverbs 31 describes a woman of unsurpassed noble character. She is the Wonder Woman of biblical proportions! She's a supermom, a hero, the perfect wife and mother. Who can live up to her standards?

Her worth is far more than rubies. Her husband is fully confident in her because she brings him good, not harm, all the days of her life. She's a wise and frugal shopper; she enjoys working with her hands. She's an early riser, readying her household for the day, cooking and serving. She's also a businesswoman who purchases property to plant vineyards. And she makes a profit! She gives to the poor and ensures her family is properly attired with the clothes and bed linens that she sews herself—usually into the wee hours of the morning. Oh, she also sells the garments she sews and supplies merchants with sashes. Her personal attire is strength, dignity, wisdom, faithful instruction, and a sense of humor. She's not lazy, and her kids and husband praise her! (As well they should.)

Even June Cleaver of *Leave It to Beaver* pales in comparison to this ideal wife and mother. But what is this passage really saying? Are we to encompass all of these virtues? How does one go about doing that?

Obviously, all the ideals mentioned in Proverbs 31 are not attainable to any one woman all of the time. Yet as Christian women, we seek to serve God, our families, and others with the gifts and resources He has given us. When our lives are centered on Christ, we are dedicated to our families, and we have a compassion for those in need. In time, we are on our way to achieving many of the characteristics of that amazing virtuous woman!

God's Snowfall Touches Our Lives

*Shun youthful lusts and flee from them,
and aim at and pursue righteousness (all that
is virtuous and good, right living, conformity
to the will of God in thought, word, and deed).*

*I*t's early morning and you've noticed that it's
just begun to snow. One of the first real snowfalls
of the season. You run to the window and linger
momentarily to watch snowflakes, like fluffy white
feathers, float gently to the ground. Calmness and
serenity envelop you.

There is something celestial about fresh-fallen
snow, as the ground is blanketed in a cloak of pure
white as far as the eye can see. Everything is touched
by its coming; even the ugly, unsightly eyesores vanish
beneath glistening white.

Soon snowplows, footprints, and tire marks
obscure your panoramic scene, leaving the snowy

mystique marred with dirt and slush. That's what happens whenever we disrupt the beauty of God's work.

When Jesus came to earth, He blanketed our world with His love and forgiveness. Through His sacrifice, He transformed the most ugly, most undesirable among us. No matter how much we have sinned, He still beckons: "Come. . .I will make them as white as snow" (Isaiah 1:18 NLT).

That is what Timothy reminded the early Christians. He admonished them to avoid the slush of youthful lusts and conform to the will of God in thought, word, and deed. He reminded them, and us, to pursue "all that is virtuous and good," all righteousness and right living.

We can learn something from winter's first snowfall. God's intervention with us always results in beauty, while our interference with or avoidance of God's will results in ugliness and sin.

Jesus came, and like pure-driven snow, our lives are forever touched by His coming.

Know the Author: Read the Book

"But I did find this: God created people to be virtuous, but they have each turned to follow their own downward path."

ECCLESIASTES 7:29 NLT

Nellie was a young woman who envisioned God as a stern, unmerciful tyrant. Troubled and confused, she found it difficult to believe that God loved her, let alone loved her unconditionally. Her uninvolved, self-absorbed, dominating dad had tainted her concept of men in general. So she questioned: *How could God love me?*

Sadly, our past influences our future whether for good or bad. God created us to become women of virtue, dedicated to His service. Yet sometimes our past gets in the way of following God's will. The enemy of our soul whispers lies in the corridors of our minds, and when we wrongly believe him, we spiral downward.

Charles Finney, a nineteenth-century revivalist said: "Do not set yourselves down to imagine a God after your own foolish hearts, but take the Bible and learn there what is the true idea of God. Do not fancy a shape or appearance, or imagine how He looks, but fix your mind on the Bible description of how He feels and what He does and what He says." Good advice!

Every woman knows that the best way to get to know someone is to talk with him or her, or read what they have written. Only when we open the book and read its contents do we discover the true character of the author. The same is true with our God. The more we ingest His words, the more we know Him. Despite our backgrounds or past experiences, God can change us in an instant and continue to instill in us the virtues He created us to possess.

Faith Is a Virtue of Excellence

For this very reason, adding your diligence {to the divine promises}, employ every effort in exercising your faith to develop virtue (excellence, resolution, Christian energy), and in {exercising} virtue {develop} knowledge (intelligence).

2 PETER 1:5 AMP

*Y*ou're determined. *This time, I will get in shape!* So you make every effort to do just that. You maintain a healthy diet; you frequent the gym and push beyond your physical limits. You stick to it with the diligence of a worker bee gathering pollen. Over time, you see results as the weight decreases, your energy soars, and your confidence grows. What sweet reward!

Exercising our faith is a similar process. As the above scripture notes, we need diligence to employ every effort to exercise our faith. It's hard at times, especially when seemingly insurmountable problems lurk like a lion awaiting its prey. But the more we exercise our faith, the more virtue grows, producing Christian excellence and energy. We become equipped to face the upcoming days, weeks, and years with more zeal and strength than we ever thought we could achieve. We learn more about ourselves and our God through our difficulties. We seek Him, knowing He is trustworthy and faithful despite how it may appear at the time.

Jamie's mom had undergone several serious operations in the span of one year. Recently, she learned that her mom needed another one. Angry and sad, Jamie tearfully embraced her mom and asked, "When will it ever end, Mom?"

Her mom, a godly woman, responded, "In God's time. Meanwhile, don't cry; rejoice, I'm in His hands."

Faith is an attribute of virtuous women. And exercising it in the face of repeated adversity is achieved through the adversity itself.

Survive, Thrive, and Bloom

But as for that {seed} in the good soil, these are
{the people} who, bearing the Word, hold it fast
in a just (noble, virtuous) and worthy heart,
and steadily bring forth fruit with patience.

LUKE 8:15 AMP

With the coming of spring and the arrival of warmer weather, have you ever noticed a lone marigold blooming in barren soil? How did it get there? What happened to make the flower bloom again when all the other annuals had wilted and died during the winter months?

Somehow the seed from that one marigold survived winter's blast and yielded a solitary flower as the warmth of the soil and sun nourished it to life.

Jesus used a parable to which most could relate in both biblical and modern times. If you've ever gardened, you understand the process. After you overturn the soil, add a little fertilizer, mark off the rows with string, and hoe an inch-deep furrow, it's time to plant the seeds. With proper watering and sunlight, tiny shoots pop up from the soil in no time. But the plant is far from bearing vegetables. A true gardener is patient as she tills, weeds, and waters. Each phase of plant growth is exciting as the first ear of corn forms, a tiny bean dangles from the vine, or a miniature green pepper emerges. As the summer progresses, the crop matures, and finally the gardener enjoys the fruits of her labors.

The Master Gardener labors over us in much the same way. He cultivates the unplowed soil of our hearts and plants the seed of His Word. Then He waters it daily with His love. But if we refuse to allow God to work, the devil will snatch the seed, or God's words will fall on a hardened heart and the pleasures of this world will choke His message.

Nevertheless, God applauds the woman who "holds fast" to His words with a virtuous heart because, like that solitary flower, despite all odds she flourishes.

Unfair?

For the righteous LORD loves justice.
The virtuous will see his face.

PSALM 11:7 NLT

*U*nfair!" your teenager spouts as she stomps out
of the room. You shake your head in dismay. *Ugh,*
you muse, *she just doesn't get it.* At different levels of
immaturity, our kids seldom understand when we
deny their requests or correct their shortcomings.
They fail to perceive what we already know because
they think they know better. What we do, we do for
our kids' benefit. We look ahead; we reason; we listen;
we assess things and determine what's best for them.

Our righteous God does the same with us. He is
just and fair. Yet we, His children, often stomp off
in a huff when we don't see answered prayer or when
life takes a wrong turn. *Why me?* we wonder. *This is
so unfair.* Yet our loving Father always has our best
interest in mind. Nothing can separate us from His

love (Romans 8:35-37). But like our own kids, we are unable to view the whole picture; as a result, we wonder if God cares or if He's listening. And if He does care, then why did this happen?

Virtues don't appear overnight. They are wrought in trials, seemingly unanswered prayers, and through a determined, dedicated, fervent, heart in the child of God. Virtues are birthed when we take the helm and redirect it away from our carnal nature.

William Penn once said: "To be innocent is to be not guilty; but to be virtuous is to overcome our evil inclinations." When *our* face is set to allow God to work in our lives without question, we will see *His* face.

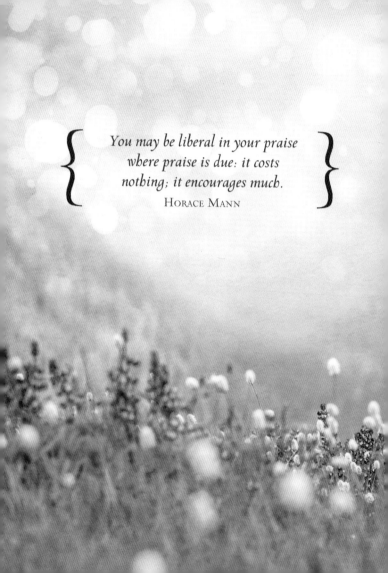

*You may be liberal in your praise
where praise is due: it costs
nothing; it encourages much.*

HORACE MANN

Give Praise Where
Praise Is Due

*First, I thank my God through Jesus Christ
for all of you, because {the report of} your
faith is made known to all the world
and is commended everywhere.*

ROMANS 1:8 AMP

It's nice to receive a compliment or be given credit for something you did. Appreciation is appreciated. When our motives are pure, we perform good deeds from a sincere heart, not for the purpose of praise. Yet to receive recognition is a blessing.

We understand the importance of praising our toddler when he or she takes that first step or speaks that first word. We praise our kids for making that field goal or raising their grade point average or remembering their manners. But why do we skimp on praise for our peers? Why is it so difficult to compliment someone else? What holds us back?

Throughout his letters to the churches, the apostle

Paul was known for his instruction, correction, and faith. Yet he was also an encourager. He gave credit where credit was due, as the above verse expresses. The church in Rome gained a reputation for their faith, and Paul recognized and praised them for it.

English composer Thomas Adams commended Peter and Paul saying: "It was well done of Paul to reprove Peter to his face, and it was well done of Peter to praise Paul in his absence."

Christians are God's voice of correction but also of cheer. We encourage the discouraged; we uplift the downtrodden; we help the helpless; we bear one another's burdens; we support, love, and give praise when praise is due. We are God's cheerleaders.

If a friend needs advice, we speak the truth in love; if she accomplishes a goal, we joyfully praise her. If she diets and loses weight, we compliment her.

Perhaps someone you know has been down and they need a boost. Although you should avoid insincere flattery, applaud and uplift her from your heart—even if it's simply admiring her new outfit!

Do you need encouragement? Remember you are unique in your gifts and abilities. Share those virtues with others, and praise liberally!

Consideration
Is Praiseworthy

Let everyone see that you are considerate in all you do. Remember, the Lord is coming soon.

PHILIPPIANS 4:5 NLT

*E*va's son recently graduated with honors from a top-notch university. At an open house she saw Dora, an acquaintance, whose son of the same age dropped out of college and lived at home, jobless. Dora was devastated.

As Eva and Dora chatted, Beth approached them, saying, "Eva, I heard about your son! How proud you must be." How do you think Eva should have responded? Let's be honest, most of us would jump at the chance to brag about our kid's accomplishments. After all, we *are* proud. But knowing how Dora felt, Eva suppressed her expressions and replied: "Thank you so much, Beth. Hey, have you met Dora?"

Eva could have gushed with facts and conversation about her successful son and his future plans, but she considered Dora's feelings. That was a commendable act on her part.

As Christian women we must exercise sensitivity. Is that woman facing adversity? If she is crabby, do we contemplate what might have happened before she came to the event? Do we consider that she may not feel well or is perhaps struggling with problems or illness? Do we give her the benefit of the doubt? Or do we mumble, "What in the world is wrong with her!" and shrug her off?

A wise person said, "You never really understand a person until you consider things from his or her point of view." In all we do we are to demonstrate a caring, considerate attitude. It truly is a praiseworthy attribute.

Trials: Pure Joy?

*Consider it pure joy, my brothers and sisters,
whenever you face trials of many kinds.*

JAMES 1:2 NIV

To the world, this verse is ridiculous. Consider it joy when you face adversity? You're kidding, right?

This is how James opened his letter to the Jewish Christians living outside of Palestine, believers among the first converts in Jerusalem who were scattered due to persecution. Think about it: These men and women suffered severe persecution unlike anything we would experience today. Their persecutors didn't just verbally degrade them for their faith in Christ; they beat, imprisoned, and killed them. Yet in all of this James encouraged these praiseworthy Christians to consider their trials pure joy.

Jesus warned us that in the world we would have tribulation. Our trials come in different forms. For some, it might be financial deprivation and the loss of their home and livelihood. Another might experience the loss of a spouse or a child. Many have marriage problems or difficulties with their children. Health problems debilitate some to the point of surrendering to physical restrictions, losing the ability to perform the tasks most of us take for granted.

C. S. Lewis said: "God, who foresaw your tribulation, has specially armed you to go through it, not without pain, but without stain." Isn't that the core of our convictions and the cornerstone of our faith? We all face tribulation, but God equips us to go through whatever hand life deals us. Stainless, we endure, secure in His hands.

Our trials benefit us; they strengthen our character and build our faith as we depend on Jesus alone. We learn we can trust and praise Him no matter what. And we have the assurance that our heavenly home awaits after our work here is done. That's when God will bless us with our richest rewards.

But for now, consider your trials pure joy. In time, God will give credit where credit is due.

Let It Shine!

Let your light so shine before men that they may
see your moral excellence and your praiseworthy,
noble, and good deeds and recognize and honor and
praise and glorify your Father Who is in heaven.

MATTHEW 5:16 AMP

We sing the Sunday school song with our children;
we proclaim it from the pulpit; we desire to attain it:
let the light of Jesus shine through us.

Think about what happens when a storm knocks
out your electricity. Without warning, the TV and
the lights go black. You grapple to find a flashlight
or a candle to light. Amazingly, one match strike
illuminates a darkened room. Jesus likened his
followers to lights shining in a dark world. If we don't
shed the light of Jesus, then who will? Yet our glow
often dulls in the frustrations of daily life.

Have you ever patiently waited for someone to
back out of a parking space, only to have another

driver whisk in front of you to get the space before you do? Do you kindly allow him, or do you seethe? In other words, is your light still on?

Or imagine you're in a hurry to return an item before work. Haphazardly, the store clerk checks the item while chatting with her coworker the whole time. Minutes seem like hours. You tap your foot and check your watch and wait. She scans the item and presses numbers into a keyboard. Then the phone rings. She answers the phone, placing your transaction on hold while she checks on an item that the caller requested. How's your lighting?

Jesus never promised that walking in the Spirit would be easy, but it is doable. He empowers us to shine despite the stark realities of darkness and aggravation. The result of our godly glow in the midst of adverse circumstances is that people notice because our positive or gracious actions or reactions are noteworthy and commendable.

The world notices women who walk in the Spirit, and the result is that God is glorified. So hide your light under a bushel? No! Let it shine.

Pass on Praises

We will not hide them from their children,
but we will tell to the generation to come the
praiseworthy deeds of the Lord, and His might,
and the wonderful works that He has performed.

PSALM 78:4 AMP

A grandmother chats with her grandchild, sharing
stories about her relationship with Christ and what
He has done for her through the years. A mom drives
her children home from school, sharing how God
answered prayer that day. An aunt visits her nephews
and nieces, and as she plays and converses with them,
she interjects how the Lord worked in her life and how
He performed miracles throughout the Bible.

The psalmist repeatedly instructs us not only
to praise God but to pass along His wonderful
works to future generations. Teaching our kids godly
principles and precepts of the Word isn't optional;
it's a command. As mothers, grandmothers, or
aunts, it is our solemn obligation not only to instruct

and emulate God's characteristics but to share our testimonies of how God intervened in our lives, or how He answered a prayer that seemed beyond the scope of possibility, or when He performed the miracle of transformation through salvation.

Gina prayed for her young son who was diagnosed with scoliosis. The severe degree of curvature meant he would need a body brace or more. Gina laid hands on her son and prayed daily. Following one test, the doctor's office phoned to say the boy needed retesting. "The results show only a slight curvature. That's inaccurate." Praising God, Gina knew better. Sure enough, the second test showed that God had healed her son.

Sharing the amazing work of the Holy Spirit will build our children's faith so that they, too, will learn to depend on Him. And when the time comes, they will continue to pass along the praiseworthy deeds of the Lord to the next generation.

Author William Tiptaft wrote: "If you had a thousand crowns you should put them all on the head of Christ! And if you had a thousand tongues they should all sing his praise, for he is worthy." God is worthy of all our praise. So speak much and sing boldly about Him! He deserves and is due our praises and more.

Royalty:
Princess and Praises

But you are a chosen people, a royal priesthood,
a holy nation, God's special possession, that you
may declare the praises of him who called you
out of darkness into his wonderful light.

1 PETER 2:9 NIV

You are royalty. That's right. God adopted you into
His family, and you are His very own. Chosen. His
special, precious possession. God set you apart from
the world.

In the Old Testament the "priesthood" was
restricted to a qualified minority. Few individuals
could make contact with God. Now, through Christ,
the priesthood is for all believers. We all have access
to God through Jesus. We offer our sacrifices to
Him through our obedience and nonconformity to
the world's ways. We serve Him with our hearts and
a willing spirit. We give because He gave. We praise
Him because He is the source of everything that is

good, righteous, and meaningful to our lives. We praise Him because of who He is.

If we could only see ourselves as God sees us. Although we often disapprove of what our children do, we continue to love them. God loves us unconditionally. We don't have to do anything to make Him love us more. We just have to surrender our hearts.

As we watch our little daughters or grand-daughters play princess, we smile with endearment and joy. As they twirl, dresses swirling and hair flowing, we embrace them with loving eyes. "Mommy, will you help me with my tiara?" our princess asks. "Of course, my sweetie," we reply as we attach it securely to her head. "There now, my royal princess, you are ready for your throne!"

Though hard to perceive, God views every Christian woman as His princess, part of His royal priesthood, equipped to perform her royal duties. You are special because the King chose you as His daughter. You gain favor because you obey Him; you are praised because you praise Him; you are loved because He first loved you. You are royal.

Commendable Faith

*Now faith is confidence in what we hope
for and assurance about what we do not see.
This is what the ancients were commended for.*

HEBREWS 11:1–2 NIV

Sandy is such a strong Christian," Abby whispered
while she attended the funeral of Sandy's husband. Left
with two young children after the sudden death of her
husband, Sandy's world was shattered in an instant.
Only a year ago, she'd lost her mother. Now this.

Plagued with grief, Sandy inwardly questioned:
How will my children and I live? What can I do
to support them? How will I ever make it without
my loving husband? Days after the funeral, Sandy
immersed herself in God's Word and prayer. She
wasn't always a woman of faith, but through the years
her trials had strengthened her in ways even she failed
to comprehend.

God had rescued her before, He would do it

again, and she knew it. She believed what God said was true. That He would sustain her–that He was a "very present help in time of trouble," just as the scriptures promised. And she stood firm despite her reservations, fears, and uncertainties.

As she walked with God, God walked with her. It was evident in her life. It wasn't that she never experienced self-pity and daily frustrations, but at the end of the day she vowed to keep her eyes on Jesus.

Due to Sandy's strong witness of faith in the face of adversity, other women came to know Christ. She taught Bible studies and spoke often of God's love and grace. And she was known and commended for her faith.

None of us know when the winds of adversity will uproot our lives and test our faith. But trials will come. The question is: Will we break under the force or bend with the wind and continue to stand? When we can't see, faith gives us sight.

Readiness Is Praiseworthy

*Strength and dignity are her clothing and her
position is strong and secure; she rejoices over the
future {the latter day or time to come, knowing
that she and her family are in readiness for it}!*

PROVERBS 31:25 AMP

Becky often quoted her favorite motto: "Think ahead
and be prepared!" Her children knew it so well that
as soon as she opened her mouth, they'd recite the
phrase. She managed her household with love and
efficiency, ready for anything. "You'd better take a
jacket," she'd instruct her teenage son, "the temper-
ature is supposed to drop." Packing for a day trip was
an event, as she brought items "just in case." Sure
enough, that Band-Aid came in handy, as well as the
lightweight blanket. Hand wipes, a change of clothes
for her small children, sunscreen, and snacks were a
must. Her family knew she'd always come through.
"Don't worry, Mom has it."

Some of us might think, *Yikes, living like that would drive me crazy.* And for some it would cause more stress than it's worth. But for Becky, going the extra mile for her family's needs was not only rewarding, it gave her a sense of security and peace.

A good president knows that our country must remain in a constant state of readiness in case of attack or emergency. A corporate executive thinks ahead and considers the prospects of advancing the corporation.

God praises readiness, too–we should be ready to serve when He asks; ready to help others; ready to provide a loving and safe environment for our kids; ready to respect our husbands even when we disagree with them; ready to meet Jesus when He finally calls us home. "Be prepared and think ahead!"

She Gave Her All

But Jesus said, Let her alone; why are
you troubling her? She has done a good and
beautiful thing to Me {praiseworthy and noble}.
Mark 14:6 amp

*W*hat a waste! That could have been used to feed
the poor!" That's what some of the people expressed
when Mary, with an alabaster jar filled with expensive
perfume, poured the costly contents over Jesus' head.
But Jesus rebuked the faultfinders. Mary's act was an
expression of her deep devotion to and profound love
for the Lord. She ministered to Him, and He praised
her so highly that He declared: "I tell you the truth,
wherever the Good News is preached throughout the
world, this woman's deed will be remembered and
discussed" (Mark 14:9 nlt).

Mary was due God's praise; extravagance was no
issue for the woman who gave what treasure she had
to anoint and bless her Master. A waste? No way.

What Mary did was a demonstration of her trust, faith, love, and commitment to Jesus.

Do we give Jesus all we have? Do we tithe our earnings and give beyond our tithes to the Lord's work and service? Would we part with our most precious heirloom or prized possession to willingly surrender to Jesus? Could we give Him *everything*, including our families, our homes, or our careers?

This is what Mary exemplified when she poured her treasured perfume over the head of Jesus. She did, in Jesus' words, a "beautiful thing." Throughout Jesus' ministry He went about doing good wherever he traveled. He healed the sick and lame, raised the dead, cast out demons, preached and taught the good news of the Gospel, and the most sacrificial act of love was that He, being perfect, died for sinners. Yet who ever ministered to Him? Mary performed a genuine, heartfelt act of love and appreciation. And because of it, Jesus not only praised her but declared that her one act of ministry to Him would be proclaimed throughout the world. Jesus gave praise where praise was due.

Imperfect Yet Praised

> By faith Abel brought God a better offering than
> Cain did. By faith he was commended as righteous,
> when God spoke well of his offerings. And by faith
> Abel still speaks, even though he is dead.
>
> HEBREWS 11:4 NIV

We all seek personal recognition. We want others to like us, and Christian women especially seek God's approval. We desire to please Him; though often we miss the mark.

But know this: pleasing God is not a matter of perfection. Who is perfect but God? No, the Lord examines the heart to assess our motives and thoughts. Are they in alignment with our deeds, or do we have ulterior motives?

Cain offered sacrifices, just as Abel did, but Cain displeased God. Cain's ways, thoughts, and motives were false and evil. On the other hand, Abel's sacrifices were birthed from a pure heart, a desire to obey and serve the Lord.

In 1 John 3:11–12 we read that God commended Abel for his faith and dedication. Eventually, due to jealousy, Cain murdered his righteous brother.

John Quincy Adams said: "A desire to be observed, considered, esteemed, praised, beloved, and admired by his fellows is one of the earliest as well as the keenest dispositions discovered in the heart of man." But like Cain, some take it too far and push for recognition at any cost. They care more about themselves and how they appear than simply living for God.

Do you desire the praise of men and God? Then allow the Holy Spirit to work in your heart to develop the characteristics that please God. Avoid jealousy, envy, and hatred, and embrace righteousness. Cultivate pure motives and a clean conscience. Some may or may not like you, but the One who really matters will be well pleased.

{
*Where the mind goes
the man follows.*
JOYCE MEYER
}

Seriously. . .
Think about It

For as he thinketh in his heart, so is he.

PROVERBS 23:7 KJV

So how's your thought life? Thinking on whatever is lovely and all the attributes of Philippians 4:8 is achievable, but no one promised a smooth ride to the paradise of positivity. In fact, few of us demonstrate positive thinking all of the time.

Problems arise that throw us off kilter; circumstances surface that confuse and cause pain. Perhaps you came from an abusive relationship, experienced a heart-wrenching divorce, the passing of a loved one, a continuum of financial drain, a chronic illness, or worse. Circumstances that are beyond our control often influence how we view life in general. We pray, and if we don't see instant results we sulk as Satan infiltrates our thoughts with lies. *God doesn't hear you! You'll never get out of this! No one cares about you!*

The late motivational speaker Zig Ziglar advised:

"We all need a daily checkup from the neck up to avoid the stinkin' thinkin' which ultimately leads to hardening of the attitudes."

The Bible warns us to guard against what we allow into our minds. The familiar axiom "You are what you eat" applies to our spiritual life as well–what we think about most translates into who we are and how we act.

Repeated negativity produces cynicism, distrust, intolerance, anger, and more. Over time, our stinkin' thinkin' will create a hardened heart toward others and toward God.

But don't give up. Although we walk in a sinful world, God will replace our stinkin' thinkin' with an attitude of gratitude!

Childish—Seriously?

*When I was a child, I spoke and thought
and reasoned as a child. But when I
grew up, I put away childish things.*

1 CORINTHIANS 13:11 NLT

Some adults, perhaps even those well into middle
age, never quite grow up. She still pouts or whines
whenever she doesn't get her way. Although he has
a wife and kids, he still leaves them at home to go
"play" with his friends. These people think and behave
like teenagers instead of grown, mature adults.

Paul expressed how we should think and act as
believers in Christ. Being childlike is depending on
God, no matter what. Being childish is immaturity.
Does that mean we become so serious-minded that
somber and boring become our middle names?
Absolutely not! Christians should be the happiest,
most joyful people in the world, even in the worst of
circumstances.

Consider Paul and Silas who overcame their circumstances with prayer and praise as they sat in a prison cell, shackled. They passed the time joyfully, praying and praising God as the other prisoners listened. The result? God loosed their chains and the prison doors opened.

Putting aside our childish ways is growing up in the Lord so that our thoughts transform from childish to mature. Mature adults are responsible; mature Christians set their minds on Christ.

When we think about the virtues outlined throughout this book, we must seriously consider them and meditate, resolve them in our minds, and deeply ponder these attributes in order to put them into practice.

Are you growing in Christ? Have you banished your childish ways?

Nature Doesn't Worry, Why Do We?

And why take ye thought for raiment?
Consider the lilies of the field, how they
grow; they toil not, neither do they spin.

MATTHEW 6:28 KJV

*W*omen are worriers by nature. And often nature
turns troublesome.

Of course, there are always the exceptions, but
women are typically the primary caregivers, home
managers, housekeepers, chefs, chauffeurs, teachers,
babysitters, and school volunteers. Amid our
plethora of duties, nature offers rain, a hardy dose
of precipitation to the mix. When the unwelcomed
downpours drench our lives, our minds race,
wondering, *Yikes! What's next?*

For a moment, relax and imagine that—in desperate
need of a reprieve—you venture outdoors for a solo
exploration of a wooded path, which leads to a cove
overlooking a sparkling mountain stream. You sit on a

hollow log near the water's edge, watching the crystal water dip and splash over boulders protruding from the rocky floor.

As you watch creation keep perfect cadence with its Creator, you are eager to hear from God. "Is there anything You want to teach me, Lord?" Then you notice that no one tells the squirrels where to find acorns; no one commands the tree branches to reach upward; no one forces the wildflowers to bloom or the water to flow downstream. No one but God, and creation complies.

This is what Jesus taught in Matthew 6. He asks, "Why do you dwell on so many meaningless matters and worry so much? If I provide for nature, I'll take care of you."

The Lord desires for us to think about His Word and dwell on the magnitude of His love for us. Sit and reflect on that awhile. Ah. . .serenity.

> *We demolish arguments and every pretension*
> *that sets itself up against the knowledge of*
> *God, and we take captive every thought*
> *to make it obedient to Christ.*

2 CORINTHIANS 10:5 NIV

*N*ancy received a callback after her annual mammogram. Her first thought? *They found a cancerous mass!* Sabrina received a voice mail from her child's school, requesting a meeting with her. Her first reaction? *Is my son in trouble? Is he lagging behind in his studies?* Josie delivered a devotional at her church's Bible study, and afterward no one complimented her. *I must have done poorly!* she thought. *Why did I do that? I'm not a speaker!* Betty arrived at her exercise class and her friend was distant. *What did I do wrong? Why is she mad at me?*

All of these women's thoughts and concerns were unfounded. Nancy's retesting went fine; Sabrina's school requested she help with a fund-raiser; Josie learned that her devotional was well received; and Betty's friend had been in an argument with her husband just before class.

If we allow them, our thoughts run amok. Whether we know it or not, our minds are Satan's battlefield. If he can defeat us with negativity, fear, and anger, he wins.

Count on it. Negative, wrong, evil thoughts will bombard our minds, especially when we're vulnerable. Personal trials will test our faith; frustrations will diminish our self-confidence; bad news will set our minds in motion, thinking about everything from the negative to the terrifying.

We always think the worst, and the more we think, the more we visualize the worst-case scenarios. But God wants us to take those negative thoughts captive, bringing them into obedience to Christ. That means we need to think about the things that are honest, true, pure, lovely, and just.

Who's the Boss?

So, if you think you are standing firm,
be careful that you don't fall!

1 CORINTHIANS 10:12 NIV

*Y*ou're doing great! For once, everything seems to go your way as your confidence soars. You received a much-deserved raise, your children are doing well in school, you achieved your weight-loss goals and treated yourself to a new hairstyle and a massage. Your church group is thriving under your leadership, and you feel good about yourself. Certainly, there's nothing wrong with that; however, along with your renewed confidence, pride gradually slips in. You believe your faith is strong, that nothing can deter you, and then it happens: your world unravels in an instant.

Remember the sitcom *Who's the Boss?* The male housekeeper worked for a corporate businesswoman, and often their roles collided or reversed. Thus the question: Who's really in charge?

As we sail through life seemingly unscathed, we often take matters into our own hands. One day we surrender to the Lord's will with sincere humility; the next day we make decisions apart from Him. One moment we prayerfully seek His guidance and wisdom, then the next we plunge forward with our own agenda. Who's really in charge?

Abraham and Sarah waited for God's promise of a son. As Sarah's biological clocked ticked way past midnight, she sent her husband to have a child through her servant, Hagar. Ishmael was conceived, but Abraham and Sarah soon realized that their self-promoted union was apart from God's will or way. Finally, at the old age of ninety, Sarah conceived the child of promise, Isaac, but not without much self-inflicted trouble in between.

We're not so different. Our thoughts convince us to plunge ahead, despite the check God gives to our spirit. We think we're strong; we believe we're right; but our thoughts are misplaced. God warns us to think seriously before we act. So always keep in mind: Who's the boss?

And now, dear brothers and sisters, one final thing. Fix your thoughts on what is true, and honorable, and right, and pure, and lovely, and admirable. Think about things that are excellent and worthy of praise.

PHILIPPIANS 4:8 NLT

What we think and how we manage our thoughts is important to God. Throughout this book we've discovered each lovely attribute of sound, faith-filled thinking. We *can* achieve the help and encouragement we need when we set our minds on whatever is lovely, recorded in God's Word.

But it takes practice. A violinist no more strums a symphony the first, second, or third time than a child walks the moment he or she is born. Walking in the Word and thinking godly thoughts take consistency, faith, time, repetition, and yes, practice. Often lovely thoughts surface on their own, but not without an insurmountable number of unlovely thoughts to battle them. Sometimes we fail, but we simply begin again.

Paul urged us to "fix" our thoughts on the admirable attributes of Philippians 4. To fix means "to establish so solidly or strongly as to make dislodgement or change extremely difficult." The prophet Isaiah wrote: "Therefore have I set my face like a flint, and I know I will not be put to shame" (Isaiah 50:7 NIV). Determined, with unwavering resolution, we must choose to fix our wills in alignment with God's. To think as He thinks; act as Jesus did; minister as the apostles and many believers that have come after them.

Ralph Waldo Emerson put it this way: "The ancestor of every action is a thought." Positive thoughts precede productive actions. So be encouraged. You *can* experience a godly thought life. You *will* achieve whatever is lovely. Seriously think about it, and prayerfully pursue it. Whatever is lovely awaits.